The Complete Guitarist
Michael Raven

"Were I to await perfection my book would never be finished."
Tai T'ung, *History of Chinese Writing* (13th Century)

A Note to the Ninth Printing.
This book was first written 23 years ago. Much of the music is hand-written and the text was set on an office typewriter. It has been tempting to re-set everything on and have it all sleek and modern, but whenever I have suggested this to both teachers and students the universal response is: "No. It is familiar and user friendly. Leave it be."
Your wish is my command. *Michael Raven*

2 8 A
2 8 SEP 2

15

Michael Raven
Yew Tree Cottage
Jug Bank, Ashley
Market Drayton
Shropshire TF9 4NJ
Telephone: 01630 672304

Printing History:
First Printed in 1974;
Reprinted in 1974, 1975, 1976,
1977, 1982, 1987, 1991, and this,
the ninth printing in 1998

Copyright:
Michael Raven 1974 ©
All Rights Reserved

Typesetting:
Eve Raven

Printed by:
Halstan, Plantation Road
Amersham, Buckinghamshire

Distributed by:
Music Exchange (Manchester Ltd)
Claverton Road, Wythenshawe
Manchester M23 9NE
Telephone: 0161 494 9783

Front Cover:
El Majo de la Guitarra
Ramon Bayeu (1746-1793)

ISBN:
0 906114 03 9

Introduction

The purpose of this book is to provide the absolute beginner with a basic knowledge of the theory of music and to give instruction in the classical finger style techniques of playing the Spanish guitar.

The course of study presented here is based on traditional teaching methods and the studies and exercises of the Classical masters such as Carulli and Carcassi are given a prominence their success as teaching material in the past deserves.   However, a variety of musical examples from other periods are also included.   These range from transcriptions of Renaissance lute music to arrangements of contemporary popular songs. The student is thus made aware of changing fashions in melody and harmony.

This book provides a tried and tested course of study and is designed to be worked through from the beginning to the end.   However, it is recommended that in addition to methodical study the student should read ahead and in particular learn some of the common chords in advance of their introduction in the course.   This is of special value in the early stages when the task of learning the natural notes and the rudiments of music can become tedious.   There is nothing wrong with strumming a simple chordal accompaniment to popular songs, indeed there are few better ways of achieving a feeling for rhythm and a sense of having made the guitar work.

This book is a self-tutor.   You could learn to play the guitar with no other help; but it cannot be stressed enough that even a few lessons from a good teacher will be of inestimable value.   A book can instruct you but it cannot hear you play, criticise and correct.   If the services of a teacher are not available in your area, then seek out the advice and help of amateur (or professional) guitarists in your neighbourhood.   The secretaries of local folk clubs, jazz clubs and music societies will often be able to help you make contact with fellow players.

Finally this book was designed for class use in an English secondary modern school and its specific purpose is to prepare a student for the Grade IV (practical and theory) examinations of the Associated Board of the Royal Schools of Music, and Trinity College of Music, London.

Michael Raven   (Stafford, England, December 1974)

Minstrels' Pillar, Beverley.

Contents

EXAMINATION GRADE PIECES

The following test pieces have been selected from the 1976 lists of two
examining authorities; The Trinity College of Music London, and the Associated
Board of the Royal Schools of Music.   The syllabuses and full lists can be
obtained free of charge from music shops.

THE GUITAR AND ITS COMPONENT PARTS

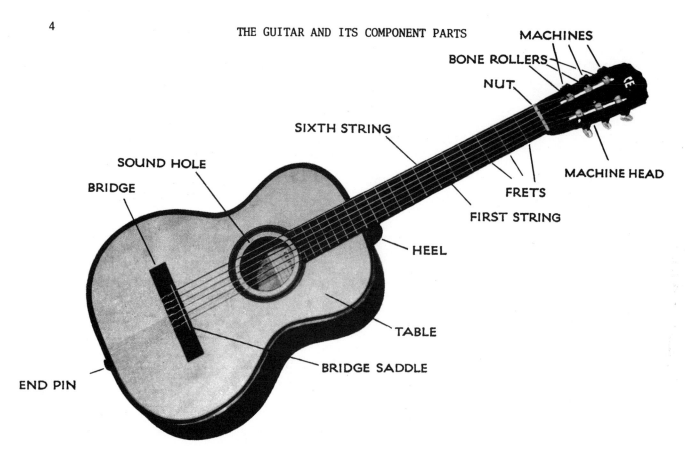

CHART OF THE SPANISH GUITAR FINGERBOARD

Below is given a complete chart of the fingerboard of the Spanish guitar. Each stave shows the notes made at every fret on that string. The student will find this invaluable for reference.

Concert Pitch

It is sufficient for practice purposes if the guitar is in tune to itself, that is that all six strings are correctly pitched in relation to each other.   It is advisable, however, to keep the strings at "concert pitch".   Either a tuning fork or a set of pitch pipes can be used to establish concert pitch.   Both only cost a few pence and will prove a worthwhile investment.   Alternatively, the guitar can be tuned to the notes of a piano.

The guitar has six strings.   The lower three (E, A and D) are always wire covered.   The upper strings (G, B and E) are usually plain nylon.   The strings are tuned to the following notes and relate to the key board of the piano thus:

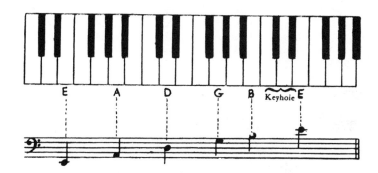

However, guitar music is always written an octave above the actual sound produced.   The notes of the open strings written according to this convention are:

Relative Tuning

Using whatever source is available bring the 1st (E) string up to concert pitch.   By turning the tuning key at the machine head we can tighten the string and so raise the pitch of the note, or slacken the string and so lower the pitch of the note.   If you have any difficulty, and almost everybody does, in judging the relative pitch, you are advised to get the assistance of a guitar teacher or musical friend.   Strings are quite expensive these days and over-tightening can easily cause breakages.

Assuming that the 1st (E) string is in concert pitch (it does not really matter if it is not exactly right), the next stage is to tune the other five strings to the 1st string. We will do this step by step.

Press 2nd string down behind 5th fret and tune to open 1st string
    ,,   3rd   ,,   ,,   ,,   4th ,, ,, ,,   ,,   2nd ,,
    ,,   4th   ,,   ,,   ,,   5th ,, ,, ,,   ,,   3rd ,,
    ,,   5th   ,,   ,,   ,,   5th ,, ,, ,,   ,,   4th ,,
    ,,   6th   ,,   ,,   ,,   5th ,, ,, ,,   ,,   5th ,,

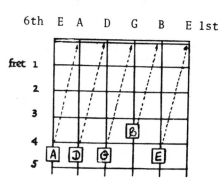

HOLDING THE GUITAR

The guitar can be held in any one of several different ways.   Which method is used is
governed very largely by the occasion and the type of music being played.   A singer
using the guitar as an accompanying instrument will often find it convenient to stand up
whilst performing.   A Classical or Flamenco guitarist will almost invariably prefer to
be seated.   Indeed, much Classical music would be impossible to perform in any other
position.   The beginner is recommended to use a sitting position whatever type of music
he or she may ultimately wish to perform.

The Classical Position

The waist of the guitar rests on the left thigh.   The left foot is placed on a foot-
stool, this has the effect of inclining the left thigh towards the body and enables the
guitar to be held down firmly between the leg and the chest.   The base of the guitar
sound box rests against the inside of the right thigh.   The neck of the guitar should
be inclined at an angle of about forty-five degrees to the floor.   This enables the
fingers of the right hand to pluck the strings at the correct angle and gives both hands
complete freedom of movement.   On no account should the guitar be supported by either
hand.

John Williams and Julian Bream

The Casual Position

The left leg is crossed over the right leg.   The waist of the guitar rests on the left
thigh.   The guitar is held to the body by the right upper arm.   This is a very natural
and convenient position but has the disadvantage of lowering the angle of the guitar neck
which can make it awkward to use the correct right hand plucking position.   Despite this
drawback this method of holding the guitar is very widely used and is a satisfactory
alternative to the Classical position.   Lady performers (even at recital standard) often
prefer this position.

Two points of some importance apply both to the Classical and casual position;(a) sit
forward on the chair, never lean back; (b) the guitar must not be tilted back to afford a
clearer view of the finger board, rather should the head lean forward.   The sound board
of the guitar should be at right angles to the floor.

The Standing Position

The guitar is supported by a strap which passes around the neck.   The right upper arm
helps to control the guitar by pressing to the body.   The hands are thus left free.
For simple accompaniment work this method is ideal.   It allows the singer freedom of
movement and facilitates breathing.   However, it is altogether unsuitable for solo
work of any complexity.

RIGHT HAND TECHNIQUE

(a)   Care of Nails

In modern finger style technique the strings are made to sound by a combination of the flesh of the tips of the finger and the nail.   The nails of the right hand are therefore of great importance.   They should extend about 1/16" beyond the tip of the finger. This should be gauged by looking at your fingers with the palm of the hand squarely facing you at eye-level.   All four finger nails should be the same length.   Any irregularity will cause one or more strings to sound differently from the others.   The thumb nail should be a little longer than the finger nails.   If your nails are too long, file them rather than cut them.   After filing the nail should be polished with very fine emery paper to remove the sharp edges, particularly on the inside edge of the nail which makes contact with the string.

Although the note is mainly made to sound by the nail striking the string it is the flesh of the tip of the finger that makes the first contact and makes a significant contribution to the final sound.

(b)   Position of the Right Hand

The fingers should strike the strings at right angles and to facilitate this the hand droops down from the wrist.   The thumb is placed out and away from the fingers.   It should not bend at the joint nearest the nail, but move as a unit.   This comes easily with a little practice.   It makes the thumb action stronger, gives more control and improves the tone.   The position of the right hand is shown in the drawings on page 8; study them carefully.

(c)   Naming the Fingers of the Right Hand

The right hand fingers are named thus:

English name	Symbol	Spanish name
index	i	indice
middle	m	medio
ring	a	anular
thumb	p	pulgar

(d)   The Rest Stroke and the Free Stroke

The fingers of the right hand can strike the strings in two ways.   Both are equally important.   Practice these strokes on the open first string using the index finger of the right hand.   To execute the Rest Stroke (apoyando) place the tip of the finger on the string to be sounded with the back of the hand tilted slightly to the left.   The finger is then drawn towards the player so sounding the string.   The finger follows through and comes to rest against the next lower string.   The finger should move from the knuckle joint and maintain a curved attitude.

To execute the Free Stroke (tirando) follow the same procedure as for the rest stroke but in this case the finger does not come to rest against the next lower string, but moves freely over it.   This is the most natural way of plucking a string.   As with the rest stroke the finger maintains a curved attitude and moves from the knuckle joint.

When changing from one stroke to the other the right hand should not alter its position. The strings should be plucked half way between the end of the fret board and the bridge. NOTE: For some time we shall not be using the thumb.   To steady the hand and to help maintain the correct position the thumb can rest on the 6th (E) string.

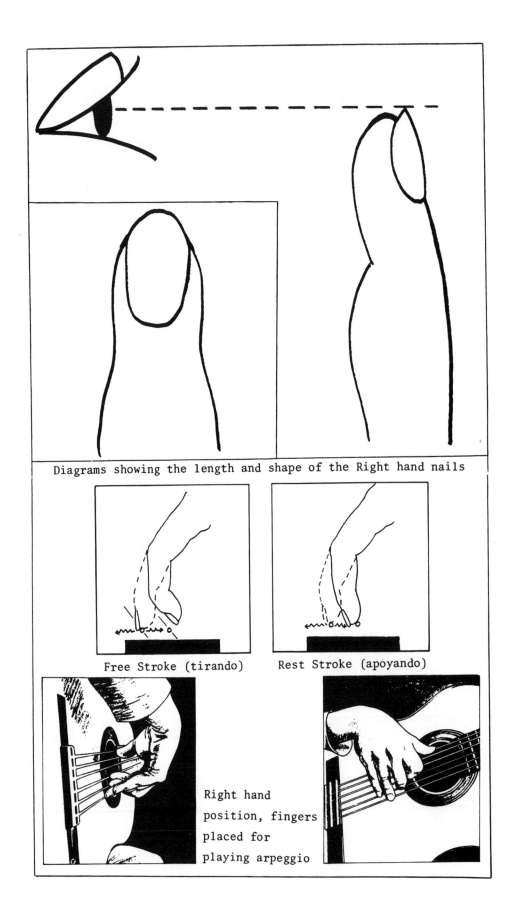

Diagrams showing the length and shape of the Right hand nails

Free Stroke (tirando)   Rest Stroke (apoyando)

Right hand
position, fingers
placed for
playing arpeggio

THE CONCEPT OF RELATIVE PITCH

Musical sounds are represented by symbols termed Notes. The pitch of a musical sound is expressed by placing a note on or between five horizontal lines called a Stave. The higher a note is on the Stave, the higher is the pitch of the sound it represents. As a tune rises and falls in pitch so do the notes that represent it on the Stave. Each line or space of the Stave has a letter name and any note placed on them takes the same name. These letter names are drawn from the first seven letters of the alphabet. More than one note can have the same name but in practice this causes no confusion.

The spaces are named

The lines are named

(Every Good Boy Deserves a Favour)

We can see at a glance that the note called G is placed lower than the note called B and if you sang the note G it would sound lower than the note B.

We will now write out in order, lowest first, all the notes we can get on the Stave:

Notes that are higher or lower in pitch are written on short lines called leger lines:

The sign  at the beginning of the Stave is called the Treble Clef, or G Clef.

This fixes the absolute pitch of all notes on the Stave. There are several other Clefs but only the Treble Clef is used in guitar music.

LEARNING THE NOTE OF 'E' ON THE FIRST STRING

If the open first string is plucked the note produced is E.

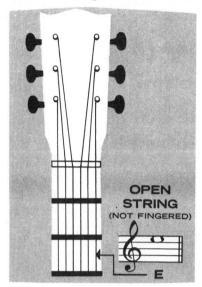

Exercises for learning the Note of E and Alternating the Right Hand Fingers

These exercises must be practised carefully.   Pay particular attention to the fingering indicated.   Before starting to play each exercise read and understand all symbols and instructions.   Use alternating fingers all the time, e.g., *i m i m* means play alternate notes with the index and middle fingers.   Remember that *a* indicates your ring finger.   To be certain that you understand how to perform both the rest stroke and the free stroke re-read the description in Lesson 1.   Properly executed these exercises will help you achieve good intonation - i.e., a pleasing and melodious sound.

Exercise 1   use the free stroke - tirando

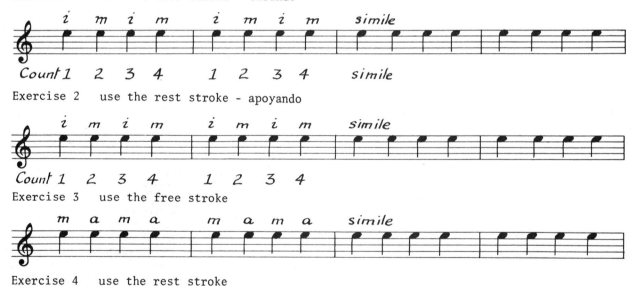

Exercise 2   use the rest stroke - apoyando

Exercise 3   use the free stroke

Exercise 4   use the rest stroke

Repeat these exercises many times.

USING THE LEFT HAND

Before we learn more notes we must prepare the left hand.   The left hand is used to
stop or hold down the strings of the guitar.   The tips of the fingers press down
immediately behind the frets, not on them.   The strings must be held down firmly or
they will rattle against the frets.

The finger nails of the left hand must be kept short so that they do not interfere with
the fingering of the strings.   Nails that are too long prevent the finger tips exerting
their full pressure and can also cause the fingers to lean over at too low an angle
which causes them to catch and "buzz" adjacent strings.

The ball of the thumb should be pressed against the back of the neck, roughly in the
middle but slightly favouring the bottom edge.   The thumb has a tendency to creep round
until it is actually gripping the top edge.   This tendency must be checked, because it
severely restricts the movement of the left hand fingers.

The wrist of the left hand should be thrust well forward, which is not possible if the
thumb is incorrectly placed, to enable fingers to drop on to the finger board from above
as nearly at right angles as possible.

The left hand should not support any of the weight of the guitar.   The entire weight
should be borne by the left thigh.

You will not appreciate the value of a lot of what has been said about both the right
and left hands until you have been playing for some time.   Wherever you get problems
look back at these pages and very often you will find a solution.

Finally, bad habits can be difficult to correct, so be correct from the beginning.   In
this early training the services of a good teacher can be invaluable.

Numbering of Left Hand Fingers

The left hand fingers are numbered thus: Index   1
                                              Middle   2
                                              Ring   3
                                              Little   4

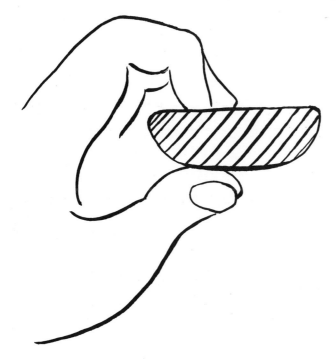

LEARNING THE NOTES OF F AND G ON THE FIRST STRING

If the 1st string is held down behind the first fret the note made is called F. If the 1st string is held down behind the third fret the note made is called G.   Thus:

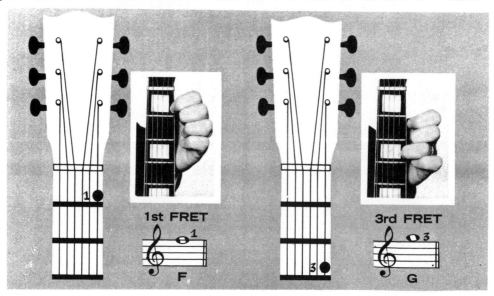

As you play the following exercises recite the letter names of the notes.

Exercise 1

Exercise 2

Exercise 3

Exercise 4

Exercise 5

THE CONCEPT OF RELATIVE DURATION OF NOTE VALUES

The relative duration of one note to another is counted in beats. The most
common one beat note is the crotchet. A note lasting for two beats is called
a minim; a note lasting for four beats is called a semibreve.

♩	Crotchet	=	1 beat	(quarter note)
♩	Minim	=	2 beats	(half note)
o	Semibreve	=	4 beats	(whole note)

BARS AND TIME SIGNATURES

Music is divided into sections or bars by bar lines thus:

Each bar contains a fixed number of beats or counts, which is indicated at the beginning
of the music by the Time Signature, for example:

The upper number tells us how many beats there are in one bar; the lower number
indicates what kind of note constitutes a beat. The beat note in this example is a
crotchet or quarter note (1/4). So 4/4 means that in the bar there are four beats, and
each beat is a quarter note (1/4) or crotchet; 4 x 1/4 = 4/4.

Likewise

means there are three beats and each beat is a quarter note (1/4) or crotchet; 3 x 1/4
= 3/4.

Exercise 1

Exercise 2

14

EXERCISES IN COUNTING TIME

Play each exercise using index (*i*), middle (*m*), and repeat using middle (*m*), anular (*a*).
Remember to alternate right hand fingers.   Use the rest stroke throughout.

Exercise 1

Exercise 2

Exercise 3

Exercise 4

Exercise 5

Exercise 6

Exercise 7

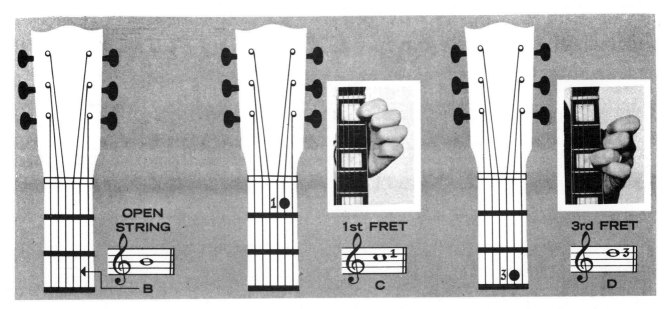

Play each exercise alternating index (*i*) and middle (*m*) fingers and repeat using middle (*m*) and anular (*a*).   Use the rest stroke throughout.   Count the time, and recite the letter name of each note.   Remember: use the index finger (1) of the left hand at the first fret, and the ring finger (3) at the third fret as marked in the music.

Exercise 1

Exercise 2

Exercise 3

In Exercise **3** note the double bar lines and the dots next to them.   The double bar line indicates the end of a section of the music, and is comparable to the full stop in ordinary writing.   The two dots are called repeat signs and mean that the music is played twice.

Summary of Notes learned so far

TUNES TO PLAY USING THE NOTES ON THE FIRST TWO STRINGS

When playing these tunes slightly accent (i.e. play a little louder), the first note of each bar. This gives the music a rhythmic pulse. Music played without a sense of rhythm sounds very dull and lifeless.

Bobby Shaftoe — English trad.

Castle Hill — M. Raven

Little John — German trad.

Dorian Melody — Michael Raven

Play the first eight bars twice and then the last four bars. Fine means End

Jingle Bells — American trad.

English Carol (extract)

What is the name of this well known tune?

French Round (extract)

What is the name of this tune?

INTRODUCING THREE-FOUR TIME AND THE DOTTED MINIM

The three-four time signature

Three-four means that there are 3 beats in the bar and that each beat is a quarter note (1/4) or crotchet. The waltz is a good example of three-four rhythm.

The Dotted Minim

By placing a dot after a note its value is increased by a half, thus:

A minim is equal to two crotchets

A dotted minim is equal to three crotchets

A dotted minim is therefore equal to three beats. Study this example:

LEARNING THE NOTES OF G AND A ON THE THIRD STRING

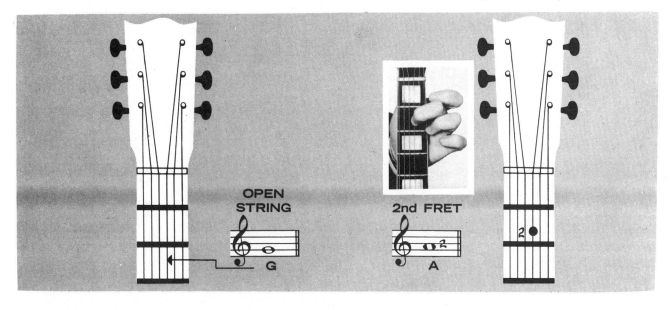

18

Summary of Notes learned so far

MELODIES USING THE NOTES G TO G ON THE FIRST THREE STRINGS

These tunes should give you pleasure to play, so practice them assiduously.   Remember: count the time.

Deep Blue Sea

Traditional

Study in Right and Left Hand Fingering

Michael Raven

To help the tune flow more easily make the G on the 1st string with the little finger (4) throughout.   On two occasions the D at the third fret on the 2nd string is also made with the little finger.   The fingering for both hands is marked, note it carefully. use the free stroke

The Streets of Laredo

American Trad

All the tunes we have played so far have started on the first beat of the bar.   They started on the count of 1.   In "The Streets of Laredo" this is not the case.   The melody begins on the last beat of a bar, in this case on the count of 3.   This is very common in song tunes and this "leading in" note is called an Anacrusis.   The last bar is a beat short to make up for the extra beat at the beginning. use the rest stroke

LEARNING THE NOTES OF D E and F ON THE FOURTH STRING

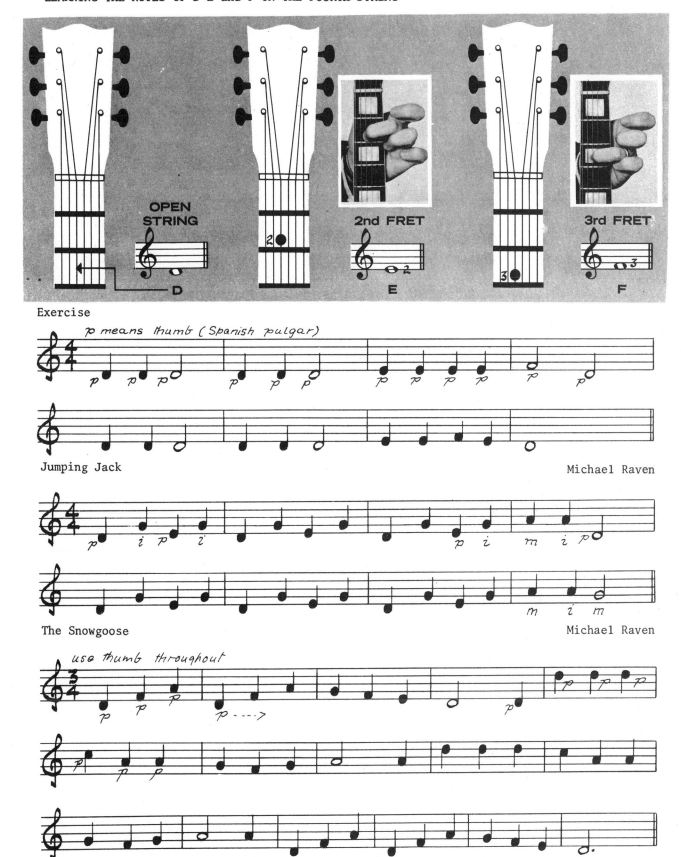

Exercise

Jumping Jack   Michael Raven

The Snowgoose   Michael Raven

INTRODUCING THE QUAVER

All the notes we have learned so far have had a duration of one beat or more.   We must now learn a new note value that has a duration of less than one beat.

This is a crotchet

If a flag is added to its stem its value is halved

This new note is called a Quaver or Eighth (1/8) note

Two   quavers are played in the time of one crotchet

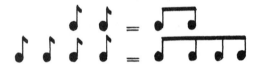

When two or more quavers are written consecutively their flags are joined together thus

When counting quavers we have to divide the count because we are now inserting notes between the main beat notes.   We usually count these "in between" notes by inserting "and" between the counts, thus:

crotchets

quavers

Remember, quavers are played twice as quickly as crotchets.

1 crotchet (1/4) note   =   2 quavers (1/8)notes

TUNES TO PLAY

Remember; when playing these tunes and indeed most of the music in this book, always slightly accent the first beat of each bar.

Skip to My Lou   American trad.

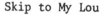

The Rowan Tree

Michael Raven

The House of the Rising Sun

American trad.

Au Clair de la Lune

French trad.

Farandole

French trad.

Frere Jacques

French trad.

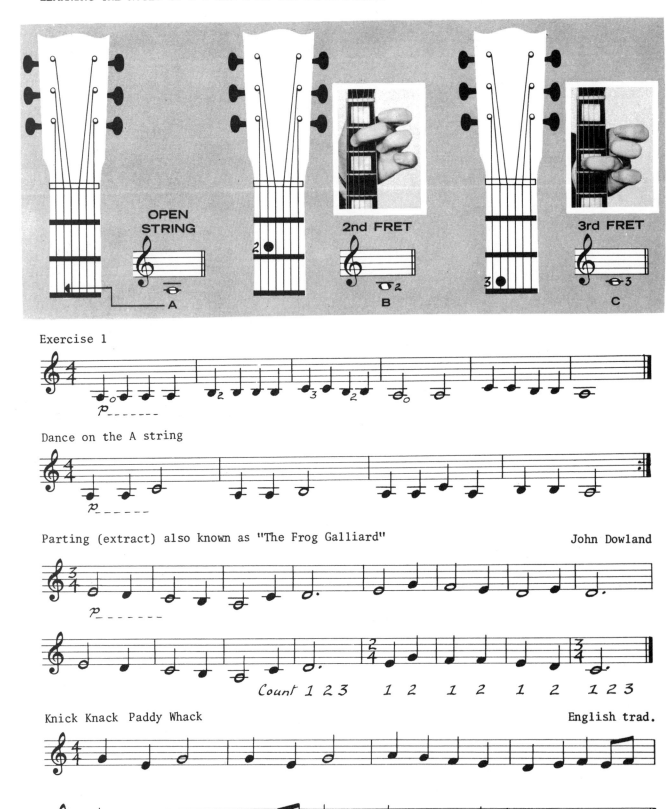

Exercise 1

Dance on the A string

Parting (extract) also known as "The Frog Galliard"   John Dowland

Count 1 2 3   1 2   1 2   1 2   1 2 3

Knick Knack Paddy Whack   English trad.

1

INTRODUCING THE SEMI-QUAVER

This is a Crotchet

By adding a flag to its stem its value is halved and it is called a Quaver

By adding a second flag, its value is halved again and it is called a Semi-Quaver, thus:

To recap.   Crotchet 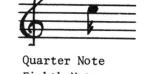   Quarter Note
              Quaver   Eighth Note
              Semi-Quaver   Sixteenth Note

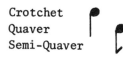

Dancing-dolls Hogarth Southwark Fair.

Like Quavers, Semi-Quavers are joined together when written consecutively.   Here is an example showing the relationship of the Semi-Quaver to the Quaver and Crotchet:

Count 1 2 3 4   1 and 2 and 3and 4and 1 a 4 a 2 a 4 a 3a4a 4a4a

What Shall We do with the Drunken Sailor   English trad.

Count 1 and a   2 and a   1 and 2 and

Morning Has Broken   Gaelic trad.

LEARNING THE NOTES OF E F and G ON THE SIXTH STRING

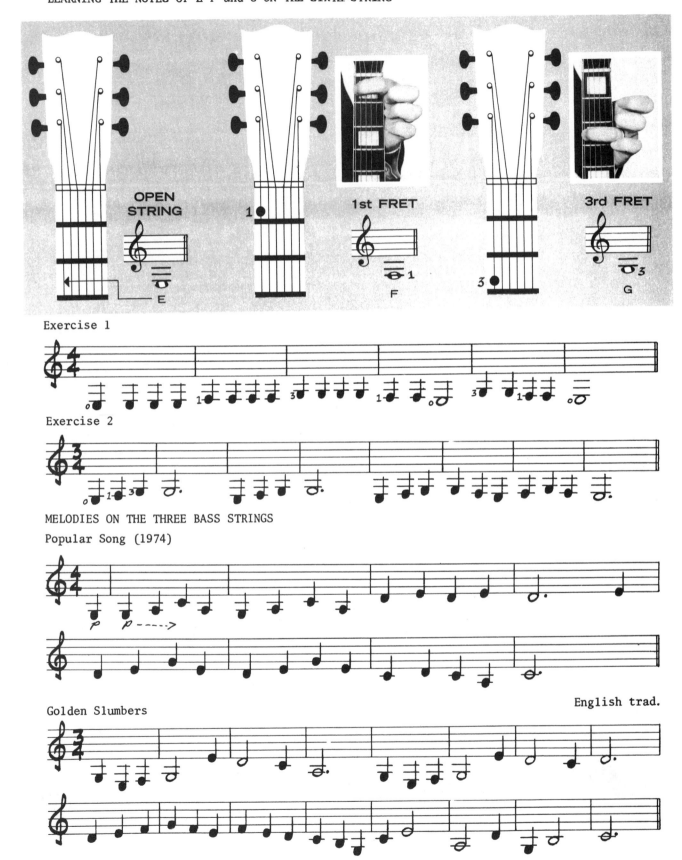

Exercise 1

Exercise 2

MELODIES ON THE THREE BASS STRINGS

Popular Song (1974)

Golden Slumbers

English trad.

Summary of the Notes learned so far

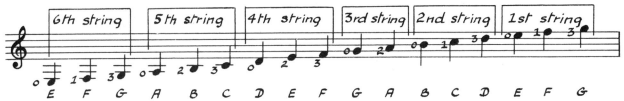

A SELECTION OF MELODIES USING ALL THE NOTES LEARNED SO FAR

Tiree Love Song.   Scottish trad.

Johnny Todd (used as the theme music for the BBC TV Series "Z Cars")   English trad.

Tallis'Canon   T. Tallis

The Holly and the Ivy   English trad.

The Scale of C Major

A scale is a series of notes arranged in a certain order.   The theory of scales is fully
discussed in a later lesson.   Suffice to say at present that scales are the basis of all
music and are therefore very important.   The scale of C Major given below must be
learned and practised every day.   You know all the notes, it is just a case of learning
them in this particular order.   Learn the scale by heart; it will make the reading of
much guitar music a great deal easier because scale passages are used very often.

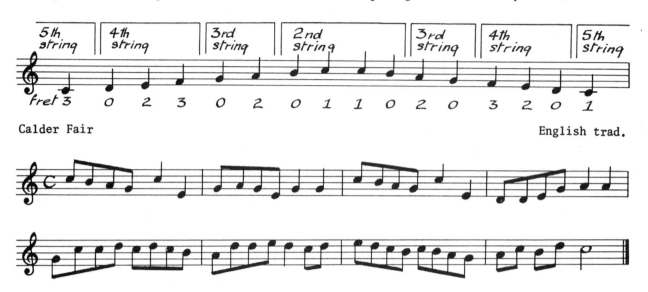

Calder Fair   English trad.

The sign C is an alternative way of writing 4/4.   Its history is this.   In the Middle
Ages 3/4 time was much favoured because the "three" linked it with the Holy Trinity.   To
indicate this "perfection" the symbol for three-four time was an unbroken circle: O
Four-four time (or common time) was then symbolised by a broken circle, to indicate its
imperfection.   A broken circle looks like a letter C and is often mistakenly understood
to be an abbreviation of Common Time.

The Can Can (from "Orpheus in the Underworld")   Offenbach

Minuet (extract)   J.S. Bach

All the music given so far has consisted of single note melody lines.   Now we must
practice playing several notes together.   It is important to have your right hand in the
correct position.   Turn back to pages 7&8 and read the instructions given.   Make sure
that all the notes on all the strings sound even and of equal strength (volume).   Pay
particular attention to the ring finger (a) because it often fails to pluck as hard as
the others.   Be certain that your nails are all the same length and have had the inside
edges polished.
                    Use the free stroke when playing the exercises on this page.

Exercise 1

Note the fingering for the right hand i = index, m = middle finger

Exercise 2

Remember: p = pulgar (thumb)

Exercise 3

Remember: a = anular (ring finger)

Exercise 4

Exercise 5

Exercise 6

Play these exercises many times

INTRODUCING RESTS

Each note value has its own rest sign, or equivalent period of silence:

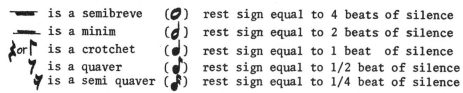

- ⎯ is a semibreve (𝑜) rest sign equal to 4 beats of silence
- ⎯ is a minim (𝑑) rest sign equal to 2 beats of silence
- 𝄽 or ⌐ is a crotchet (𝅘𝅥) rest sign equal to 1 beat of silence
- 𝄾 is a quaver (𝅘𝅥𝅮) rest sign equal to 1/2 beat of silence
- 𝄾 is a semi quaver (𝅘𝅥𝅯) rest sign equal to 1/4 beat of silence

A rest sign means silence. The strings should not be allowed to sound through a rest sign. This often means we have to damp the strings to stop them ringing out. Periods of silence are important in any music, but especially so in modern popular music where the "missing beat" or the damped note can create great rhythmic interest and excitement. Indeed, the work of many rock and folk guitarists would sound quite dull without them.

There are three methods of damping the strings:

a) By replacing the fingers of the right hand on the strings thus damping the preceding notes.

b) By releasing the pressure of the left hand fingers which hold the strings to the fretboard. This method cannot, obviously, be used on open string notes.

c) By placing the palm or the outside edge of the right hand across all strings. This is a method commonly used in flamenco music.

Method (a) is the most generally useful and is recommended for use in the following examples.

Exercise 1

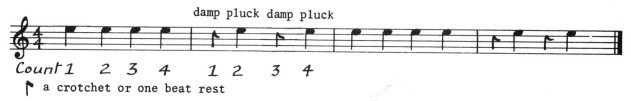

⌐ a crotchet or one beat rest

In the second bar there are crotchet rests on the first and third beats. These beats must be silent. On the count of 1 in the second bar damp the string by placing a finger of the right hand to kill the sound. (Make as though to pluck the string but don't). Repeat this procedure on the count of 3. Practice this first exercise many times to get the feel of this new technique.

Exercise 2

In this exercise replace the three fingers and thumb to damp the preceding chord. This needs a lot of practice.

NOTE: When the fingers have plucked the strings on the count of 1 keep them together as a unit so that they can fall back onto the strings easily without each separate finger fumbling for its respective string. The fingers should touch each other at the tips and stay pressed to each other.

AN INTRODUCTION TO CONTRAPUNTAL MUSIC

The basis of most Western music is vocal melody.   Originally the melody was sung by one
voice.   If other voices joined in they simply sang along with the soloist in unison.
The next step was for a second voice to sing the same melody but at a different pitch.
In church music this was called Organum.   This in turn led to the notion of having two
different melodies being sung together.   The main melody (Cantus Firmus) had a secondary
melody (the descant) written above it.   Most of us will be familiar with this idea from
school.

Once this concept of two part music was established it was developed and other voices
added.   Such "many voiced" music is called polyphonic or contrapuntal and reached its
greatest heights during Shakespeare's time.

This idea of many voices, each with its own part, was adopted by composers of
instrumental music.   Instead of voices, instruments were used.   From the 16th century
to this day instrumental music had been dominated by the concept of vocal polyphony.
Most instruments, like the human voice, can only play single note melodies so to perform
music in four parts requires four instruments.   However, we are fortunate as guitar
players because, like pianists, we can play music in two, three or four parts (or voices)
on one instrument.

To begin with though we will only play in two parts.   As an example here is a popular
melody to which has been added a second voice.

Au Clair de La Lune (in two voices)

Reading two notes together takes a lot of practice so play slowly and repeat the exercise
many times.   The melody notes have their tails pointing upwards and the notes of the
added tune or second voice have their tails pointing downwards.   The added lower voice
notes are played with the thumb throughout.   It may help you to play the two tunes
separately first.

Note the left hand fingering.   It will help you to locate the notes if you keep your
index (i) finger pressed down behind the first fret on the 2nd string throughout, even
when you are not playing that note (C).   One of the secrets of good fingering is never
to remove a finger from the fret board unless it is necessary.

Remember: when music is in two parts think of it as being sung by two voices; when it is
in three parts think of it as being sung by three voices.

Good King Wenceslas   tune: anon. 16th century arranged M. Raven

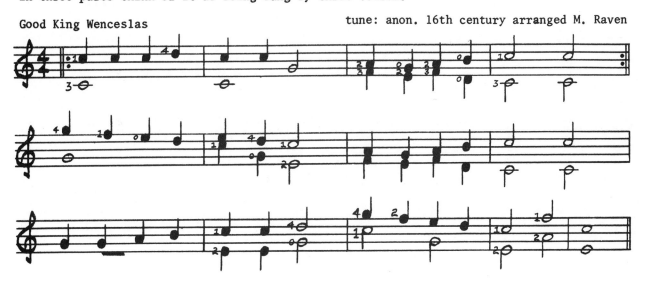

30

Andantino   Joseph Kuffner

Notes:

1. The recommended right hand fingering is shown, but any practical alternative can be
    used.

2. Note the rest signs.   The second voice is silent for the first two bars and does
    not enter until the count of 2 in the third bar.   The semibreve rest (4 beats of
    silence) is commonly used when a voice is silent for a whole bar, regardless of the
    actual number of beats (in this case only 3).

3. In the fifth bar the last note has tails pointing both up and down.   The second
    lower voice has come back in and sings in unison with the main upper melody.

4. In the sixth bar the note A is sung in unison on the count of 1.   The main
    melody then goes off to sing other notes whilst the lower voice holds the note for
    the whole bar - 3 counts.   So keep the string held down to allow the note to ring
    out.

Aire   Mauro Guiliani adapted M. Raven

Musette

Michael Raven

In this piece the tune is played by the thumb on the bass strings and the fingers
provide an accompaniment by droning on the open first string.   In Classical music
this is called pedalling and the drone note is called a pedal note.   The principle
of the drone is very old and some folk instruments such as the bagpipe and the
hurdy gurdy have drones built into them.   (A Musette is a French bagpipe).

AN INTRODUCTION TO ARPEGGIO TECHNIQUE

In the last lesson we had several examples of music in two parts. The next logical step is to add a third voice. But now the composer has to be especially careful that not only do the three tunes sound well separately but sound well played together. It needs some thought and skill to set two voices but a great deal more to set three. The composer must study theory of harmony, that is the combining of notes together. Harmony is the subject of books many times the size of this Tutor. Suffice to say at present that when three or more notes are played together they are called a chord. Chords that by themselves sound settled and pleasing are called conchords; and chords that by themselves sound unsettled and displeasing are called dischords. The basic theory of the most common chords is discussed in a later lesson; for now it is sufficient to appreciate that a chord is simply the combination of three or more different notes.

Here is an example of three part music:

The three voices have combined to form chords. We play such block chords on the guitar just as if three voices were singing. But we can also play them in a way that the human voice cannot - or at least only does as an exercise - and that is to split up the notes of the chord and play them rapidly one after the other. This is called an arpeggio. Taking the example given above we could play the chords like this:

The playing of chords in the form of an arpeggio is very common in guitar music. There are many different arpeggio patterns but some are used more often than others. Shown below are the most important. They must be practised diligently and often; slowly at first and then with increasing speed. They are the foundation of much beautiful solo guitar and are also used very extensively to accompany songs of all kinds - popular, classical and folk.

Take careful note of the right hand fingering. So that the left hand does not get tired or strained by holding down chords for long periods, these arpeggios have been written out using open strings.

Before commencing Patterns 1 and 2 place the thumb and fingers on their respective strings - i.e., thumb on the 6th string, index finger (*i*) on the 3rd string, middle finger (*m*) on the 2nd string, and the ring finger (*a*) on the 1st string. The thumb should be out and away from the fingers in the direction of the machine head. (Turn back to page 8 and study the drawing).

Each pattern must flow without interruption. Many beginners tend to pause slightly before each bass note - be conscious of this tendency and try to avoid it from the beginning.

In arpeggio 3 the bass note is only played once. The semibreve is the true note. The quaver is only added to make clear the relative duration between the first and second note of the arpeggio. Theoretically it should be (and sometimes is) written thus:

In the arpeggio studies that follow four chords are used. To help you find the notes they are spelt out below: (a) on the finger board chart, (b) as an arpeggio, (c) with the main bass note separated from the rest of the chord, and (d) as a block chord.

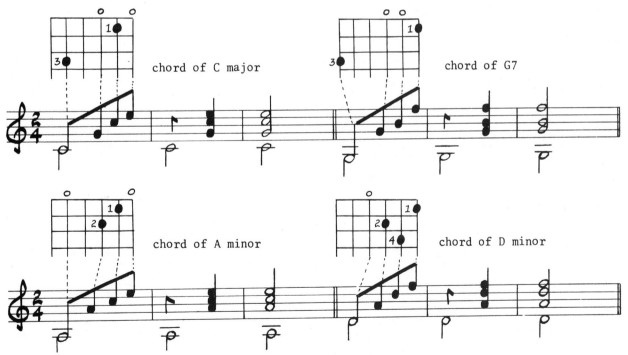

NOTE: There are fuller versions of these chords and they will be shown later. For now these shapes are all that are needed.

34

Learn to recognise the pattern the notes of a chord make on the stave.   After a while
you will come to know the pattern and thus not have to work out each individual note.
Make the chord shape necessary for a particular bar and hold it until a new shape has to
be made.   Do not remove fingers until you have to, and be certain that the bass notes
(which have their tails pointing downwards) are allowed to ring out for their full value.

Arpeggio Study in C Major   Michael Raven

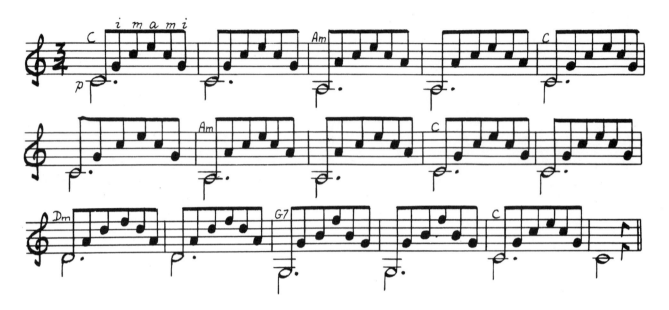

Prelude   Matteo Carcassi

(a prelude is music that precedes another piece or pieces)

Andante   Ferdinand Carulli

(Andante means "at a graceful, moderate tempo")

The preceding two studies were fairly straightforward.   There were three or four voices
in the form of chords played arpeggio.   In the following study there is more movement in
the voices.   This has the effect of making them stand out more clearly as separate parts.
The music is in three parts, or voices.   There is a bass tune; a middle part which most
of the time consists of a simple drone on the open third string (G); and a treble tune
which consists of the upper notes of the arpeggio.   The bass tune is played by the thumb
and is indicated by notes with their tails pointing downwards.   The drone and upper
melody are played by the fingers and are indicated by notes with their tails pointing
upwards.   Play the music through a few times and you will find that the parts emerge without difficulty.   Remember, the bass notes must be held down so that they can ring out
for their full value.

> is an accent sign and means play the notes so marked a little more
                                                              loudly.

A pause sign ⌢ or fermata placed under or over a note
indicates that it is to be prolonged; the duration of
the pause is left to the discretion of the performer.

It is also used to indicate the end of a piece of music.

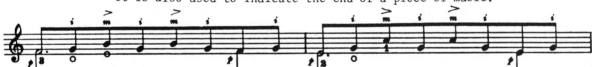

INTRODUCING SHARPS AND FLATS

All the notes that we have learned so far are what are called the natural notes. We can make other notes by either sharpening or flattening the natural notes. To sharpen a note we raise it by a semitone, to flatten a note we lower it by a semitone.

On the guitar the interval from one fret to the next is a half tone, or semitone. Thus to sharpen a note all we do is move up one fret (towards the bridge); and to flatten a note we move down one fret.

Summary

A sharp	♯	raises a note by one semitone
A flat	♭	lowers a note by one semitone
A Natural	♮	restores a note to its original pitch

On rare occasions it is necessary to raise or lower a note by two semitones. A double sharp (✗) indicates that a note is to be raised by two semitones; a double flat (♭♭) that it is to be lowered by two semitones.

Examples of Accidental Sharps, Flats and the Natural Sign.

Example 1   Example 2

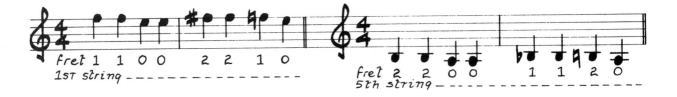

Learning the notes of F sharp and C sharp

These are not chord shapes — play the notes separately.

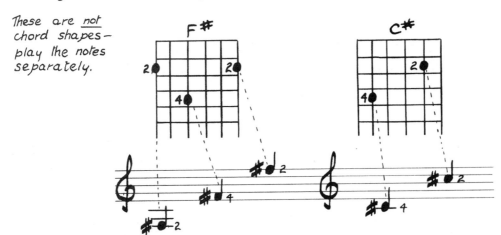

The best way to remember these notes is to realise that all we have done is play all natural C's and F's one fret higher than usual.

Important

An Accidental sharp or flat sign only affects the note against which it is written and notes of the same name and pitch that follow it in the same bar. A note of the same name and pitch in the next bar is automatically naturalised.

Study (using F sharp and C sharp)   Ferdinand Carulli

D.C. stands for Da Capo (Italian, "from the head") and means go back to the beginning of the music and start again.   Al Fine means to the end.

So D.C. al Fine means go back to the beginning and play until the end, which in this example is at the end of the second line.

Waltz Lavinia   Michael Raven

38

THE TIE SIGN

Count 1 2

The curved line in the above example is called a Tie sign.   It indicates that the first note is played and then allowed to ring out for its own value plus that of the note to which it is tied. Play the first note on the count of 1 and let it ring out through the count of 2.

Under normal circumstances we would not tie two crochets together as in our example. We would simply write a minim  which is equal to two crochets:

Why then do we have tied notes?   Consider this example.

Count 1 2 3 1 2 3

The two tied crochets are equal to a minim but we cannot write a minim because the bar line would divide the note.   So this example is played:

but has to be written:

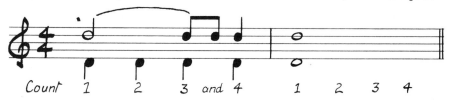

It is also sometimes necessary to tie two notes within the bar, for example:

Count 1 2 3 and 4 1 2 3 4

Because we do not have a time value sign equal to two and a half beats we have to tie a two beat note (a minim) and a half beat note (a quaver).   Study the example carefully and be sure that you understand the reasoning.

Always remember that when two notes are tied (a) only the first note is played and (b) that it is then allowed to ring out for its own value plus that of the tied note.

Study in Tied Notes   Michael Raven

The first time you play this study leave out the bass notes (tails pointing downwards)

INTRODUCING THE DOTTED CROTCHET

We are already familiar with the Dotted Minim  and the fact that a dot placed after a note increases its value by a half

The Crotchet ♩ is affected in exactly the same way. By placing a dot after a Crotchet we increase its value by a half, thus:

(two quavers)
(three quavers)

However, the musical effect on this shorter note is somewhat different. It gives a characteristic jerk to the rhythm. This is because the Crotchet is usually the beat note and by adding half a beat to its length it means that the note following it is thrown on to the off beat. This is best understood by means of an example. And what better example than the National Anthem of the United Kingdom.

This shows quite clearly that the note following the dotted crochet in the second bar has been forced on to the off-beat between the counts of 2 and 3.

In passing it might be mentioned that the National Anthem is a perfect example of the dance rhythm known as the Galliard.

French Popular Song   arranged M. Raven

THEORY OF SCALES PART ONE

The Octave

When a tensioned string is plucked the note made sounds the same as that made by plucking a string half its length, at the same tension.   The note produced by the half length string is at a much higher pitch but is otherwise identical to the first note.   These two notes are said to be an Octave apart, and are given the same name.

We will demonstrate this on the guitar.   Pluck the open 1st (E) string and let the note ring out.   Now halve the length of the string by placing a finger behind the twelfth fret (the twelfth fret lies exactly halfway between the nut and the bridge).   Pluck the string again.   The note sounds the same as the first, but at a much higher pitch. These two notes are an Octave apart and both have the same name (E).

This most perfect interval of all was known to the ancient Greeks, and is the foundation upon which all the scales of Western European music are built.

The Scale

If we sub-divide the Octave into steps or intervals we form a scale.   The "steps" we use are the Tone and the Semitone (or half tone).   On the guitar the distance from one fret to the next is a Semitone; hence the distance from one fret to the next but one is a Tone.   For example:

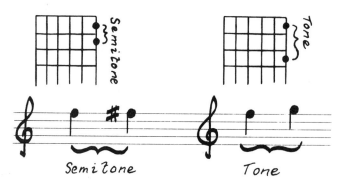

There are two main kinds of scales in use today; the Diatonic and the Chromatic.   The Diatonic (lit. two sounds) Scale consists of tones and semitones, and the Chromatic (lit. colourful) Scale consists entirely of semitones.

The Diatonic Scales

The most important Diatonic Scales are the Major scale and Minor scale.   Each scale consists of seven notes, though the ear does not recognise it as complete until the eighth note, the Octave, is added.   We will now discuss the Major scale.   The Minor scale will be dealt with in the next lesson.

The Major Scale

The Major scale is built of tones and semitones arranged in a definite order.   It is this order which makes it different from all other scales.   The sequence in a Major scale is:

TONE   TONE   SEMITONE (TONE) TONE   TONE   SEMITONE

If we build a Major scale on the note C we find that the correct order of tones and semitones is given by using only the natural notes (no sharps or flats) thus:

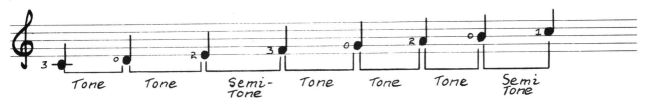

The Key Signature

All other Major scales require one or more sharps or flats to maintain this sequence of tones and semitones.

For example, if we build a Major scale on the note G we find that one of the natural notes has to be altered to maintain the sequence.

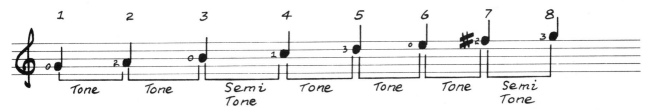

If the F had not been sharpened there would have been only one semitone between the 6th and 7th notes of the scale (when there should have been a tone) and a tone between the 7th and 8th notes of the scale (when there should have been a semitone). By sharpening the F both these errors are corrected, and the scale becomes a Major scale based on the note G. The note on which a scale is built is called the key note. In this example the note was G, and music that is written using this scale is said to be in the key of G major.

Music written using the scale of G major will need all the F's to be sharpened. To avoid having to write a sharp (#) wherever F occurs we place it at the beginning of each line of music after the Treble Clef sign. This is called the Key Signature.

Thus, all F's are automatically sharpened - not just the F on the top line of the stave, but all F's. The only way it can be cancelled and the F restored to its natural state is by using a Natural Sign (♮) against the note in the music. Sharps and flats placed in a Key Signature are called Essential. Any other sharp or flat signs that occur in a piece are called Accidental, and only affect the note against which they are written for the duration of one bar.

Major scales can be built on any note. If we build a major scale on the note D it is called the scale of D major and music written using that scale will be said to be in the key of D major.

INTRODUCING THE SCALE OF G MAJOR

Practice these scales daily. Pay special attention to the fingering of the left hand.
Remember; fourth fret use little finger (4), third fret use third finger (3), second fret
use second finger (2), first fret use first finger (1).

Scale of G major (in high octave)

Scale of G major (in low octave)

Remember: use the little finger (4) to make the note of F# (4th string, fourth fret).

The most commonly used chords in the key of G major

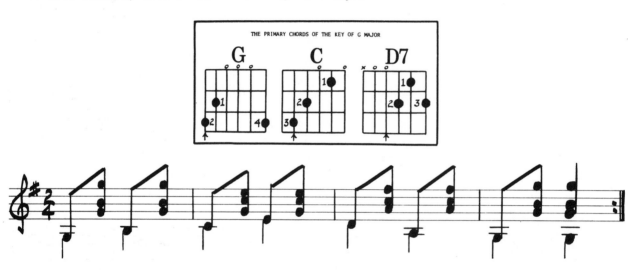

You might well find these chords quite difficult. Learn them now and practice them
often. Meanwhile you can proceed because the studies that follow do not depend on your
having mastered these chords.

D.C. (Da Capo) is Italian
for "from the head" and
means go back to the
beginning and play all
the music again.

Young Jane   Irish traditional arr. M. Raven

Sauteuse in G major   Matteo Carcassi

THEORY OF SCALES PART TWO

In the last lesson we discussed the Major scale. We must now turn our attention to
another kind of scale. It is called the Minor scale. The reason for having two types
of scale is that they each have a different sound. Music based on a Major scale has a
bold bright sound; music based on a Minor scale has a gentler, softer sound. Because of
its haunting quality the Minor scale is often used for laments and love songs such as
"Greensleeves".

The Ancient Minor Scale

The Minor scale, like the Major scale, is Diatonic. That is it is built of tones and
semitones arranged in a special order. What makes a Minor scale different from a Major
scale is the order of these tones and semitones. The sequence of these is:

TONE   SEMITONE   TONE   TONE   SEMITONE   TONE   TONE

If we build a Minor scale on the note A we find that the correct order is given by using
only the natural notes (no sharps or flats). Thus:

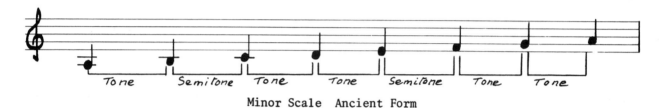

Minor Scale   Ancient Form

Minor scales starting on any other note require one or more sharps or flats to maintain
this order of tones and semitones - just as did the Major scales.

Because the scale of C major and A minor both use only the natural notes they are said to
be related. The scale of A minor is often referred to as "the relative minor of
C major", and C major as "the relative major of A minor".

The Harmonic Minor Scale

However, there is a little more that must be said about the Minor scale, because for
practical reasons the ancient Minor scale (known in the Middle Ages as the Aeolian Mode)
has been adapted for modern use.

The first change involved the sharpening of the 7th, or leading, note of the scale.
This was done principally in the interests of instrumental music. It enables harmony
to come to a satisfying conclusion by creating a semitone between the 7th and 8th notes
of the scale. Thus altered it is now called the Harmonic Minor Scale.

Minor Scale Harmonic Form

The Melodic Minor Scale

The Harmonic Minor scale was ideal for instrumental music but caused problems for singers
because the interval between the 6th and 7th notes of the scale was now one and a half
tones. Western Europeans find this interval difficult to sing though in Middle Eastern

music this interval is very common.   To overcome this difficulty the Melodic Minor scale was evolved.   The 6th and 7th notes are sharpened on ascending and returned to their original pitch on descending.   This removed the awkward one and a half tone jump.

The Minor Scale Melodic Form

The sharps and flats in the Harmonic and Melodic Minor scales are treated as accidentals, that is, they are written in the music as they occur,and are not placed in the Key Signature.

Do not be disturbed by the complications of the Minor scale.   In practice they present no problem.

Note Names of Major and Minor Scales

Each note of the major and minor scales has a name which indicates its relative importance.   Both scales use the same names, though they are illustrated here on a major scale.

Tonic	means:	key note, from Fr. and Ger. word 'ton'
Supertonic	means:	above the Tonic
Mediant	means:	midway between the Tonic and the Dominant
Sub Dominant	means:	important (dominant) but less so than the Dominant
Dominant	means:	most important (dominant) except for the Tonic
Sub Mediant	means:	midway between Sub Dominant and Octave Tonic. The Sub means it is a less important halfway note than the Mediant.
Leading Note	means:	this note 'leads', or wants resolution to the Tonic

---

Learning the note of G sharp (G♯)

The best way of remembering the note G sharp is to realise that it is a semitone (one fret) higher than G natural wherever it occurs.

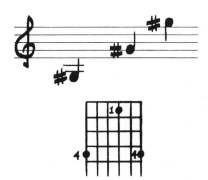

INTRODUCING THE SCALE OF A MINOR

Scale of A Minor Harmonic Form

The relative major key of A minor is C major.   The three most commonly used chords in the key of A minor are:

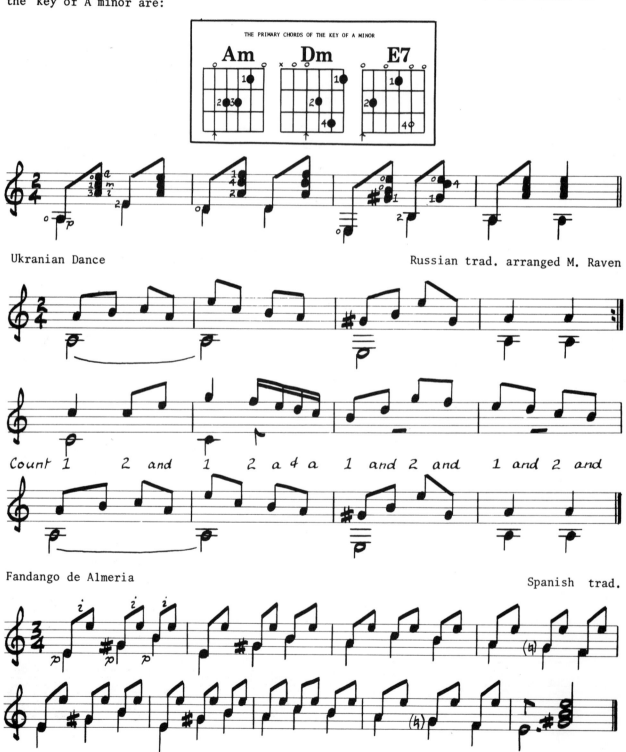

Ukranian Dance

Russian trad. arranged M. Raven

Count 1   2 and   1   2 a 4 a   1 and 2 and   1 and 2 and

Fandango de Almeria

Spanish trad.

INTRODUCING THREE-EIGHT TIME

So far the basis of all our counting has been the crotchet (or quarter note). There is, however, another family of time signature that use the quaver (or eighth note) as the "beat" note. Three-Eight for example means that there are three eighth note counts in the bar. Thus:

It is clear that three-eight time is very similar to three-four time. We still count three beats to the bar but each beat is half the value. In practice we virtually read music in 3/8 time as if it were in 3/4 time. Indeed, the same piece of music is often written both ways. A famous Waltz by Carulli for example, is written in different books as either 3/8 or 3/4 thus:

Why bother having 3/8 time then, you might well ask. There are two main reasons. First it can sometimes make the music easier to read, all the notes of one time value being joined together as in the example above; and second because it is a conventional way of indicating that the music should be played fairly quickly.

Lavender's Blue - Study in counting 3/8 time

Dance in A Minor   Michael Raven

LEARNING THE NOTE OF B ON THE THIRD STRING

The note B 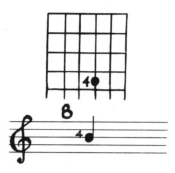 is normally made by playing the second string open.

However, in several of the pieces of music that follow it is necessary to make
this note at an alternative position that is by holding down the third string
behind the fourth fret.

To summarise: If your guitar is correctly tuned the open second string and the
third string held down behind the fourth fret produce the same note, B.   Why do
we need another way to make B you might ask.   There are several reasons.
First the two B's although of the same pitch have different timbres, or tone
colourings.

Play them and judge for yourself.   Secondly, if we wish to play the notes B and D
together thus: then it is clear that the notes must be placed on

different strings - it is impossible to play together two different notes on the
same string.

Trezza   Anonymous 17th century

Grade I group A Trinity College

This is your first test piece.   Study it carefully and practice it often.   Note
the dotted crotchets (see page 39); hold the bass notes for their full value;
watch the fingering carefully; remember to play only the first note of notes tied
together; and in the ninth bar make the B on the third string at the fourth
fret.

Important.   You are advised to memorise this piece so that you can play it without the music.   Learn the first four bars and play them over and over again until
they are fixed in your mind.   Then learn the next four bars, practice them, and
so on.

Allegretto - fairly fast

THEORY OF SCALE PART THREE

The Chromatic Scale

To most musicians the Chromatic scale is of theoretical rather than practical value.
Only very modern (atonal) music uses this scale as its base.   Most Western music is
written using either the Major or the Minor scales, though it is not uncommon to find
Chromatic passages in music based on these scales.

The Chromatic scale consists entirely of semitones.   If we take a Major scale and fill
in all the missing semitones, we have a Chromatic scale.   The missing semitones can be
written as either sharps of the notes before them, or as flats of the notes after them.
For example the missing semitone between C and D can be named either C sharp (C#) or D
flat (D♭).   Such two name notes are called Enharmonic.

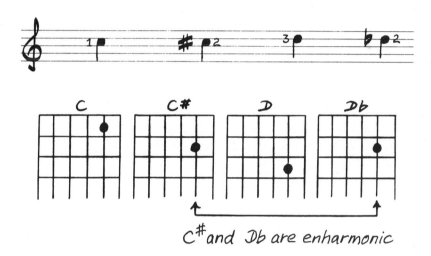

C#and Db are enharmonic

The usual practice is to write the missing semitones as sharps when ascending and as
flats when descending.   In the Chromatic scale given here the Natural notes are shown
with tails and those without have been added to make a Chromatic scale.

Chromatic Scale

Play this Chromatic scale through several times and learn it slowly, over a period of
time.

50

THEORY OF INTERVALS

Look at this figure

There are two notes.   The lower note is C and the upper note is E.   If we count the
number of natural notes between them, including the two notes themselves, we find that
they number three, thus:C D E.   The notes of C and E are said to be a third apart, and
we refer to them as "thirds".   This interval of a third is much used in Western music.
It is easy to recognise because the two notes are always on adjacent lines or spaces.

What is the interval between these two notes?

Remember, count the number of lines and spaces between them, including the lines and
spaces occupied by the notes themselves, or write out the letter names of the notes as we
did before, thus:

                    G   A   B   C   D   E

There are six notes.   The notes G and E are said to be a sixth apart, and we refer to
them as sixths.   Here is a chart showing the most important intervals.

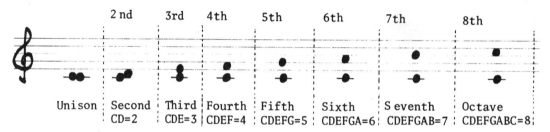

Compound Intervals

Intervals greater than an octave are called compound intervals and are calculated in
exactly the same way.   For example:

Counting the steps of the scale between these two notes - C D E F G A B C D E - we see
that they number ten.   The interval is therefore called a tenth.

Studies Illustrating the Use of Common Intervals

Waltz

Ferdinand Carulli

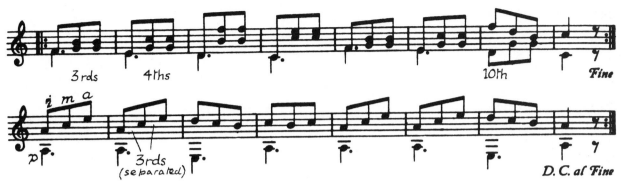

Chimes at Night   Chinese folksong arr. M. Raven

The melody is harmonised by exactly the same tune at an interval of a fourth below it. This is the oldest form of harmony known and was very common in Western Europe during the Middle Ages.   Only the intervals of a fourth, a fifth and an octave allow this singing of the same tune as a harmony.   For this reason these intervals are called Perfect. Parallel Fourths and Fifths were used in early church music - Plainsong - and in that connection were called Organum.   A tune was harmonised by adding notes either a fifth above or a fourth below.

There is one other aspect of the theory of intervals that we need to know something of before going on to discuss the structure of chords.

Major and Minor Thirds

The interval of a third can be either large or small.   When large it is called Major; when small it is called Minor: In a Major Third there are 4 semitones
                                          In a Minor Third there are 3 semitones

We can show the difference between a major and a minor third quite easily by keeping all the notes on one string thus:

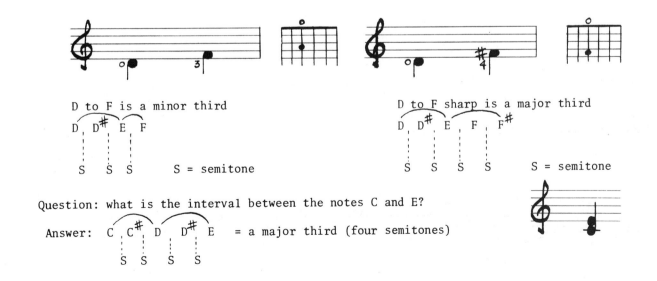

52

THEORY OF CHORDS

A chord is made whenever three or more notes are sounded together.   Of the many hundreds of chords it is possible to make only a few are commonly used.   The simplest and most important chords are the Triads based on the notes of the scale.

A Triad consists of three notes; a Root Note, which can be any note of the scale; the note which lies an interval of a Third above the Root, and the note that lies at an interval of a Fifth above the Root.

To build a Triad on the note of C we add the note that lies on the next line of the stave above C (which is E), and the note that lies on the second line above C (which is G). All three notes lie on adjacent lines thus;

The interval between C and E is a major third equal to four semitones; and the interval between C and G is a perfect fifth.

The three notes C E G are called a triad and the chord they make is named after,

and

    (a)   the Root Note, which is C

    (b)   the quality of the interval between the Root and the note a third above, which is major - i.e., a major third equal to four semitones.

The chord C E G is therefore called C major.

To build a triad on the note D we add the note that lies on the next space of the stave above D (which is F) and the note that lies on the second space above D (which is A). All these notes lie on adjacent spaces thus:

The interval between D and F is a minor third equal to three semitones, and the interval between D and A is a perfect fifth.

The three notes D F A are a triad and the chord they make is named after,

and

    (a)   the Root Note, which is D

    (b)   the quality of the interval between the Root and the note a third above, which is minor - i.e., a minor third equal to three semitones.

The chord D F A is thus named D minor.

This process can be repeated for each note of the scale. All the triads built on a major scale are either major or minor chords, except that built on the seventh note of the scale, which consists of a minor third (3 semitones) and a diminished fifth (6 semitones - a perfect fifth has 7 semitones). This triad is termed diminished.

These are the triads based on the Major scale:

Minor scales are treated no differently from major scales. During the Classical period (1750 - 1820) chords were usually built on the Harmonic Minor Scale, but today, as in Renaissance times, chords are more commonly based on the pure Ancient Minor Scale (Aeolian mode); with the exception of the Dominant V chord in which the Third is sharpened so converting what would have been a minor triad into a major triad.

These are the triads based on the Minor Scale

The Primary Triads

Three of these triads are of more practical importance than the others. They are called the Primary Triads and are those based on the first note of the scale (the Tonic, I), and the fourth note of the scale (the Sub-Dominant IV), and the fifth note of the scale (the Dominant, V). Thus

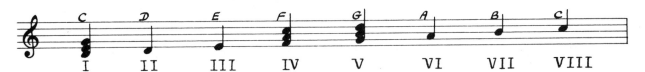

The three most important chords based on the scale of C are therefore

Chord	C Major	I	Tonic
	F Major	IV	Sub Dominant
	G Major	V	Dominant

The Chord of the Dominant Seventh V7

In practice we usually add to the triad of Dominant V the note that lies at an interval of a minor 7th from the root of the chord

In this case the root note is G and the note that lies a minor 7th above it is F. This additional note is indicated in the chord symbol by adding the figure seven, thus: G7 (V7). So, the three most commonly used chords are

I	IV	V7
C	F	G7

54

Here are two more examples:

Scale of G major   G   A   B   C   D   E   F#   (G)
                              I   IV   V

The most commonly used chords are therefore I, IV, & V7, or G C & D7

Scale of A minor   A   B   C   D   E   F   G   (A)
                              I   IV   V

The most commonly used chords are therefore I, IV & V7, or Am, Dm and E7

Practical Chords and Chord Shapes

Before we begin to use chords in a practical way there is one thing more we must understand.   We have established that this is a chord of C major
and that the three notes of a chord of C major are C E G.

Any combination of these three notes make a chord of C.   We can alter the arrangements;
E G C (which is called the 1st inversion), or G C E (which is called the 2nd inversion)
and always we have a chord of C.   We can also duplicate the notes - e.g., have two notes
of C, or two notes of G, or three notes of E.   Just so long as at least one of each of
the three notes is present it does not matter in what order they occur, or if they are
duplicated.

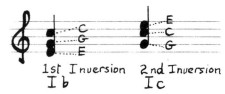

A chord in its Root position is indicated
by its Roman numeral; in its First
Inversion by the Roman numeral plus the
letter b; in its Second Inversion by a
letter c.

Some arrangements of the notes are easier to play on the guitar than others.   This, for
example, is a very common way of making the chord of C:

We can draw a diagram of the guitar fingerboard and show this common arrangement of notes
quite clearly.

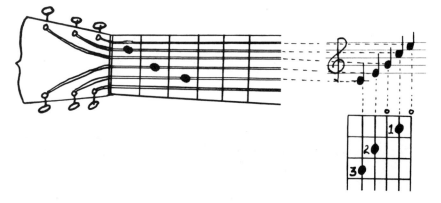

The numerals indicate which finger of the left hand the black dots represent.

Andante

Fernando Sor

Grade I group B Trinity College of Music examination

Take care to hold all notes for their full value. Do not overlook
the tie signs (see page 38). Before playing this piece practice
the following exercise which will prepare you for the music of the
second, third and fourth lines.   The interval between the pairs
of notes is a tenth.

AN INTRODUCTION TO SONG ACCOMPANIMENT

The guitar is an ideal instrument with which to accompany songs.   It has a gentle unobtrusive sound that blends well with the human voice.

Most songs can be effectively accompanied by the use of first position chords and simple rhythms.   Most collections of popular music and folk songs have the chords marked above the melody line.   Here we will discuss how to use these chords to make effective accompaniments.

The simplest accompaniment, and one which properly executed can be most effective, is to strum the strings rhythmically with fingers of the right hand, changing chord as necessary.   (In flamenco this rhythmic strumming is called Rasgueado and has been developed to a high degree).

However, we will begin by using right hand patterns in which the thumb plucks a bass note and the fingers pluck either a block chord or play the notes of the chord separately in the form of an arpeggio.

The first song to which we will fit an accompaniment is "Skip to my Lou".   We will sing it in the key of C major, so the chords will be those based on the scale of C.   The three Primary chords for the key of C major are   I   IV   V7
                                                                                                          C   F   G7

Here are chord diagrams showing these chords in their most common practical 'shapes'.

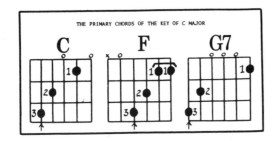

An X means that the note made on that string does not belong to the chord.   It should not be played.

(NOTE: The F chord shape is quite difficult and needs a lot of practice, but it is a very important shape and must be mastered).   The bracket indicates that the index finger lies flat and holds down two strings.   Be careful <u>not</u> to flatten the second and third fingers as well or they will deaden adjacent strings.

In fact we only need two of these chords to accompany "Skip to my Lou" - namely C and G7. The right hand pattern we will use is a straightforward "thumb pluck", in which the thumb plays a bass note and the fingers pluck the treble string notes of the chord thus

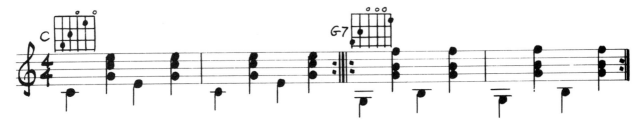

Note that the thumb plays two different bass notes.   This is called alternating the bass. Practice this pattern on the two chords as shown above to familiarise yourself with it before applying it as an accompaniment to the song.   In particular practice changing from one chord shape to the other.   It may be several days before you can play the accompaniment and sing the song together - but persevere - and be certain to keep a regular, steady rhythm.   It is no good stopping at each chord change.

Skip to my Lou

As an introduction repeat the first bar of the accompaniment a few times.

An alternative to the bass chord pattern we have just used is this arpeggio (with which you should be familiar).

Practice the following exercise to establish the relationship of the two patterns.

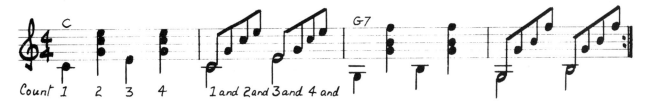

On page 84 of this book there is a selection of well known songs with suggested chord symbols. Use them to practice the common chords and arpeggios. There are few better ways of making more enjoyable what can be a tedious task.

58

INTRODUCING THE KEY OF E MINOR

All F's are sharpened

Scale E minor Ancient Form

Scale E minor Harmonic Form

Scale of E minor Harmonic Form - lower octave.

Scale E minor Melodic Form

The key of E minor is the relative minor of the key of G major.

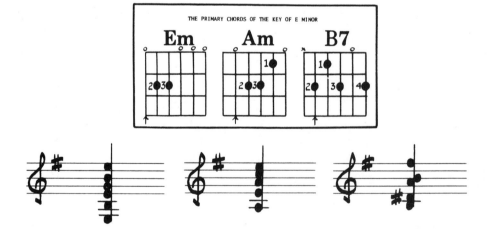

Tonality

= slightly arpeggio chord by running thumb across it from 6th string to 1st string

The Position and Introduction to "Cossacka" by J. Kuffner

The fret at which the index finger holds down a string determines the position of
the left hand.   If the index finger holds down a string behind the first fret we
are playing in the First Position.   If it is placed at the second fret, then we
are in the Second Position, and so on.   Positions are indicated by Roman
numerals I, II, etc.

In the Cossack dance below we are called upon to change position from the first to
the third fret.   In preparation for this play the following exercise:

The first bar commences with the notes G and B played on the open strings.   The A
and C are made with the index finger at the first fret (1st string) and the second
finger at the second fret (3rd string).   Keeping this shape the two fingers
slide up two frets - the index finger to make the note D on the 2nd string and the
2nd finger to make the note B at the fourth fret on the 3rd string.   There is no
need to take the fingers off the strings as they change from the first position to
the third position.   They glide up pressed to the strings.   This is indicated by
the lines joining the notes.

Cossacka   Joseph Kuffner adapted M. Raven

Count the time

Waltz in E Minor

Ferdinand Carulli

Grade I group B Trinity College.

3rd finger remains on 1st string 2nd fret for bars 3 and 4

LEARNING THE NOTE OF A ON THE FIRST STRING

If the first string is held down at the 5th fret the note
made is A. The note A is written on the first leger
line above the stave.

A 1st string
5th fret

God Rest Ye Merry, Gentlemen

Traditional arranged Michael Raven

First play the melody by itself; then add the second voice, tails pointing down
wards. The complete piece will need a lot of practice. You can proceed to the
next pages but keep returning until you have mastered this music.

Bates.   R. Winter. C. Wright. J. Wright.   Percy.   Fawkes.   Catesby.   T. Winter.

Key A minor

Andante in A Minor

Ferdinand Carulli

mp	means mezzo-piano, moderately soft
f	means forte, loud
Dal Segno 𝄋	means from the sign; go back to the sign and play again
	means gradually increase the volume
	means gradually decrease the volume

INTRODUCING THE DOTTED QUAVER IN THREE-EIGHT TIME

The Dotted Quaver is equal to three semi quavers.   Thus:

We have already mentioned the similarity of three-eight time to three-four time.   The effect of a dotted quaver in three-eight time is the same as the dotted crotchet in three-four time.

This can be made perfectly clear by writing out the National Anthem in three-eight time thus:

Count   1   2   3   1 2 and 3

The National Anthem is usually written in three-four time, but a good example of a tune that is conventionally written in three-eight is "Greensleeves".

Greensleeves   Anon. 16th century English

INTRODUCING SIX-EIGHT TIME

Six-Eight is another time signature that is counted in eighth notes (or quavers).
Six-Eight means that there are six eighth notes or their equivalent in one bar.
These notes are grouped into "threes" thus:

The first note of each group of three is accented.

Slow six-eight and Fast six-eight

There are two kinds of six-eight time - fast and slow.

Music in slow 6/8 time is counted  the beat is the quaver

Music in fast 6/8 time is counted  the beat is the dotted crotchet

This duality of six-eight time might seem confusing but in practice causes little
difficulty. If you sing a fast six-eight tune like "Pop Goes the Weasel" you
instinctively tap two beats to the bar. If you sing a slow six-eight tune such as
"Drink to me only with Thine Eyes" you automatically tap 1 2 3, 1 2 3 - i.e., six beats
to the bar. Here are some examples that should make this clear. (Bear in mind that if
you play these examples on the guitar you may well play fast six-eight tunes too slowly
at first because of technical limitations).

Drink to me only with Thine Eyes (slow 6/8)

Girls and Boys Come out to Play (fast 6/8)

Pop Goes the Weasel (fast 6/8)

Andantino in C Major   F. Sor

Melody in G Major   adapted from D. Aguado

LEARNING THE NOTES OF THE SECOND POSITION

With the index finger at the second fret the hand is in the Second Position.   To
complete our knowledge of the second position it is only necessary to learn the
notes at the fifth fret.

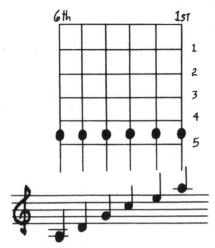

You will notice that with the exception of A on the 1st string we have already learned
all these notes, but not at this location.

1. The note on the 1st string at the fifth fret is A

2. The note on the 2nd string at the fifth fret is E = same as open 1st string

3.   "   3rd   "   fifth "   C = same as 2nd string first fret

4.   "   4th   "   fifth "   G = same as open 3rd string

5.   "   5th   "   fifth "   D = same as open 4th string

6.   "   6th   "   fifth "   A = same as open 5th string

These alternative locations of the same notes should give you little trouble because
you are very familiar with all but two (A on the 1st string and C on the 3rd string)
from tuning your guitar.   Remember that and there is no problem.

There are two reasons why we must learn to make the same note on different strings.

1.   The same note played on two different strings has different tone colourings.
     Make E  by plucking the open 1st string.   Now make it by holding

     down the second string at the 5th fret, just as you do when tuning the guitar
     The E on the second string has a softer, richer sound.

2.   Play these notes

You will see that it would be impossible to play the note A on the first
string and the note E on the first string together.   So we have to make the
note E on the second string.   Note that in guitar music we indicate which
string a note is to be played on by a number in a circle :

    ① means 1st string
    ② means 2nd string
    ③ means 3rd string, and so on

THE SCALES OF C MAJOR AND A MINOR USING ONLY 'STOPPED' NOTES

These scales use no open strings. The index finger is at the second fret;the hand
is in the second position. Note the fingering carefully. Practice these scales daily.
In ascending scale it is recommended that the fingers are held down after a note has
been sounded and then taken off all together when moving to the next higher string.
This procedure aids legato playing (legato - smooth, flowing).

Scale of C major

Scale of A minor

These two scales are required for the Grade I examination of Trinity College. They
must be memorised. Candidates also have to play the notes of the chords of E minor
and G major in the form of an arpeggio to the extent of one octave

Scarborough Fair   English traditional arr. M. Raven

In bars 7, 11 and 21 the notes C and E of the A minor chord have to be made on the 3rd
and 2nd strings.   Note the tie sign in bars 7, 8 and 14.

68

INTRODUCING THE KEY OF D MAJOR

Note the key signature, all C's and F's are sharp.

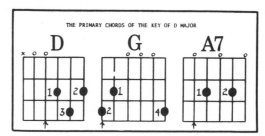

The relative Minor Key of D major is B minor.

Eight Bar Polka   Michael Raven

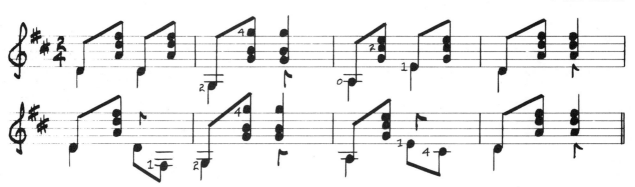

Rondo (extract)   Ferdinand Carulli

Passamezzo Moderno

anonymous 16th century
adapted and arranged by M. Raven

To play this piece it is necessary to retune the 6th string by lowering it one tone to
D. It will then sound an octave lower than the open 4th string. If you have retuned
correctly the 6th string held down at the seventh fret should sound in unison with the
open 5th. This tuning is very common and is indicated at the beginning of the music by
the string number in a circle and the instruction "to D". Occasionally other strings
of the guitar are required to be retuned for special effects. For example " 5 to G"
means retune the 5th string to the note G - i.e., lower it one tone.

The passamezzo moderno (It. passo e mezzo = at a pace and a half) was a brisk dance of
the late 16th and early 17th centuries. The passamezzo moderno was in a major key, the
passamezzo antico (old) was in a minor key. It was a lively form of the Pavan, which
was a slow, dignified walking dance.

Note the time signature. The broken circle (C) means that there are four crotchets to
the bar. The line crossing it means that though there are four crotchets to the bar
there are only two beats. This has virtually the same meaning as 2/2. There are
therefore two minim beats in each bar.

see p.70

70

INTRODUCING THE TECHNIQUE OF LIGADO

(a)   The Ascending Ligado (Hammering-On)

When two notes are linked together by a curved line at the dot end of the note thus:

then the second of the two notes is played ligado (or slurred).   In the example above the procedure is as follows.   Play the open *fourth* string to make the note D ring out.   Then hammer the second finger of the left hand down on to the fretboard behind the second fret. The second finger must come down hard from above and at right angles to the fretboard. The second note, E, should then sound quite clearly without having been plucked by the right hand.   You might not get it right the first time, but practice it and you will find it comes quite easily.   Here is another example:

The index finger of the left hand makes the note F at the first fret.   The string is plucked thus sounding the note.   The third finger of the left hand then hammers down hard to make the note G sound out.

(b)   The Descending Ligado (Pulling-Off)

In the above example the first note G is made by holding down the 1st string behind the 3rd fret with the third finger of the left hand.   The string is then plucked and the note of G is made to sound.   The third finger of the left hand then pulls off sideways (away from you towards the floor) and actually plucks the string as it does so.   The left hand plucks the string and so makes the note of E sound out.

In this example

we follow exactly the same procedure, but in this case the index finger must be positioned at the first fret in readiness.   This means that the third finger and the index finger will be on the fretboard together.   It is important that the index finger be pressing the string very firmly so that the string cannot move when the third finger pulls off.

Ligados are used for three reasons. First, when properly executed they "slur" the notes together; the notes merge into one another more than when plucked separately. Secondly when playing scale passages the use of hammering-on and pulling-off can considerably increase speed and ease the load on the right hand plucking fingers. Many of the runs used in flamenco guitar music, for example, would be virtually impossible without ligados. Thirdly, ligados are often used quite deliberately for rhythmic syncopation.

It is not uncommon to have to hammer-on or pull-off several notes at one time.

For example:

In both these examples only the first note is plucked by the right hand. In example (b), the left hand fingers hammer-on and then pull-off in one flowing movement.

Ligado Study

This exercise demonstrates and provides practice for most of the ligado techniques. At the point marked (A) note that you hammer-on from the off beat note to the on beat. This is a very characteristic rhythmic syncopation for which the slur is used. At the point marked (B) note that only the first of the four notes, F, is actually plucked; the E and D are made by pulling-off and the E the second time by hammering-on. This is difficult to perform at a slow tempo but will become much easier as your speed increases.

Landler   Joseph Kuffner

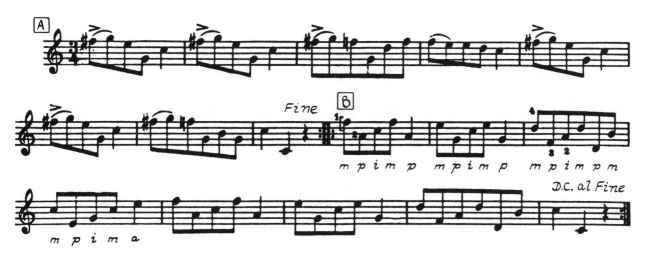

D.C. (Da Capo) al Fine means "From the beginning to the End". The end (Fine) is the end of the first section of the music. The two sections of the music have been marked (A) and (B). The playing order of this piece can be written (including repeats) AA BB A. When playing Da Capo repeat signs are ignored, so the repeat of A at the end is only played once.

soon

INTRODUCING THE ACCIACCATURA

Acciaccatura (from Italian acciaccore = to crush)

The acciaccatura is a grace note that has no fixed time value.   It is played very
quickly and in effect borrows time from the note that follows.   It is always played
ligado - i.e., it is always either hammered-on or pulled-off.

To play this example first pluck the open 1st string and hammer the index finger down
at the first fret as quickly as you can after having plucked the string.   The index
finger must really snap down hard.   The same thinking applies when a grace note is
pulled-off, for example:

The index finger must pull-off the first fret as quickly as possible.

When a bass note is written under the main note it is played with the grace note.

written   played   or to be exact

My Lady Vals   Anon. arr. M. Raven

THE DOTTED QUAVER IN FOUR-FOUR AND THREE-FOUR TIME

One of the most common dotted quaver figures in 2/4, 3/4 or 4/4 time is this. The first note has a duration of three semiquavers, the second only one semiquaver thus:

Now play this example very slowly whilst counting the time.

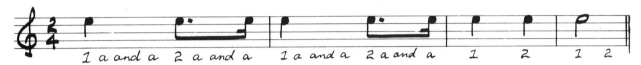

In practice of course we do not count the time of such short note values. With a little practice we feel the rhythm of this figure and play without really thinking. The best way to acquire the knack is to play through a few well known tunes that use this figure and make a conscious effort to relate the sound to the way it is written. Finally, this brief summary might be of help to you:

Tannebaum (this tune is also known as "The Red Flag")

Rock of Ages

INTRODUCING THE KEY OF A MAJOR

All C's F's and G's are sharpened

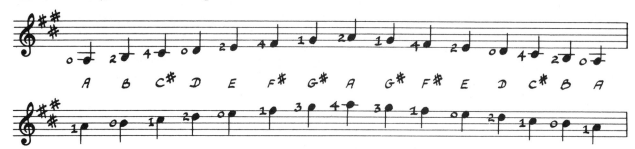

A   B   C#   D   E   F#   G#   A   G#   F#   E   D   C#   B   A

Scale of A major in Two Octaves

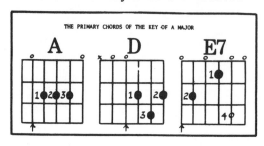

The relative Minor Key of A major in F#minor

Tonality

Prelude   Carcassi adapted Raven

Wilson's Wilde
Anonymous

Wilson's Wilde is an anonymous Renaissance dance.   The Renaissance period roughly coincides with the reign of the English queen, Elizabeth I.   The tune was popular then, and became widely known in recent years when it was used as the background music for a television advertisement for English cheese(!)   It is technically easy but should be played at a fastish tempo.

The tune has three themes.   Each theme is followed by an ornamented variation.   It is suggested that the themes are played legato, with a singing quality; and the variations rather more harshly and staccato.

INTRODUCING THE TECHNIQUE OF BARRÉ

Barré means bar.   It refers to the technique of holding two or more strings down with one finger.   With rare exceptions it is the index finger that executes barré.

Full barré, or Great Barré, is when the index finger is laid across all six strings.

Half Barré is when the index finger is laid across anything less than all six strings, i.e., two, three, four or five strings.

Barré is indicated in guitar music in several ways.   (In these examples the index finger is positioned at the 3rd fret).

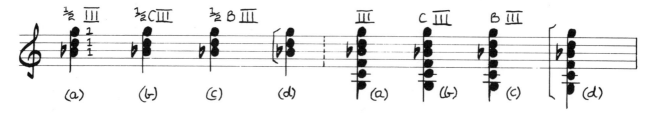

The fret at which barré is to be made is usually indicated by Roman numerals I, II, III, IV, etc.   If barré has to be held the duration of the hold is usually marked by either a line or dotted line, thus

Barré is an important technique.   It enables the guitarist to play combinations of notes that would otherwise be impossible.   Most beginners have little difficulty with the half barré, but full barré needs constant practice.   At first it may seem impossible to hold all the notes down without getting buzzes and rattles but practice makes perfect.   Do not practice barré chords for too long at any one time.   The hand gets tired and you will become frustrated.   As every individual's hand and finger length is different it is difficult to offer advice except to say that the wrist must be thrust forward and out-wards so that the index finger can lie flat on the fingerboard with all joints locked keeping the finger straight.   Perhaps the best chord with which to practice Great Barré is the F major chord (six string version) at the 1st position, thus:

Studies in Barré
Study No.1

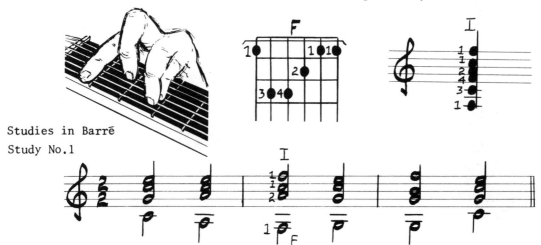

Study No.2

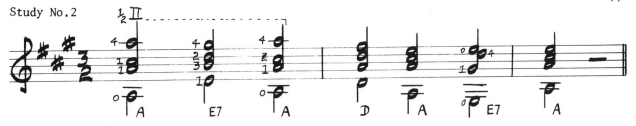

Study No.3

The common chords of the key of B minor (relative minor of D major)

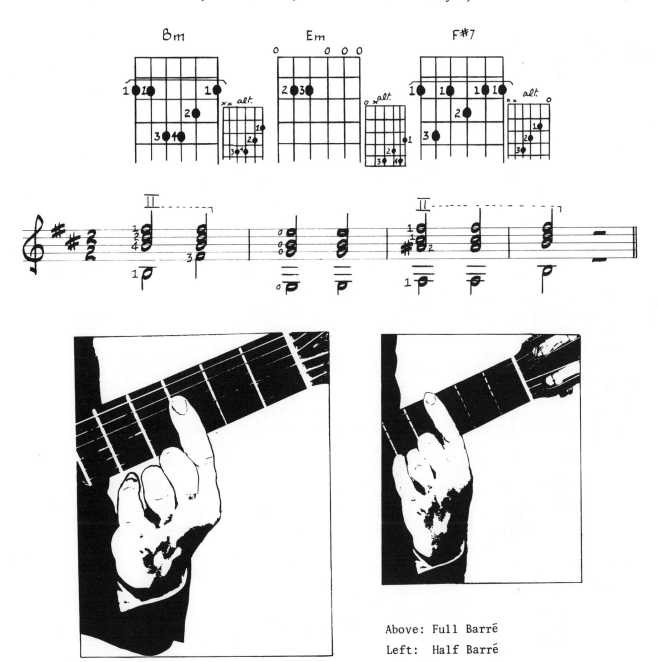

Above: Full Barré

Left: Half Barré

INTRODUCING THE KEY OF F MAJOR

All B's flattened

The relative minor key of F major is D minor

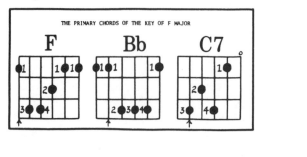

Tonality

Poco Allegretto   F. Carulli

This study consists of chords played arpeggio linked by scale runs.   Remember, all B's are flattened except when restored to their original pitch by an accidental natural sign.

INTRODUCING THE KEY OF D MINOR

All B's flattened

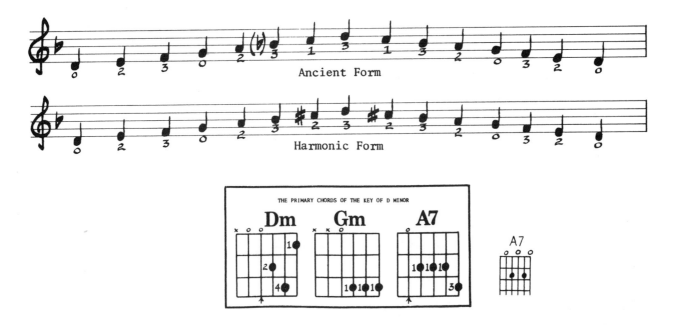

Ancient Form

Harmonic Form

Danza de las Hachas   Anon 17th century arr. M. Raven

The Hatchet Dance is an old Spanish tune that was used by Joaquin Rodrigo in his Fantasia
para un Gentilhombre, for guitar and orchestra.

INTRODUCING THE KEY OF E MAJOR

All F's C's G's and D's are sharpened

The relative Minor of key of E major is C sharp minor

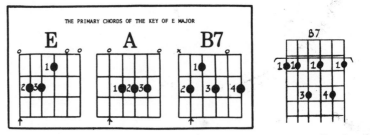

Study in E major   F. Carulli

Riff in E   M. Raven

Hold a chord of E throughout.   Add the little finger for the C#, and lift the index
finger for the G♮ .   Note the hammering-on

Holy Night, Silent Night   Franz Gruber arr. M. Raven

Minuetto   Robert de Visee

Group A grade II Trinity College
Robert de Visee was court guitarist to "The Sun King", Louis XIV of France.
The minuette was a moderately paced dance especially popular in the 18th century.

Andantino

Matteo Carcassi

Group B grade II Trinity College

84

SKIP TO MY LOU

```
C
Skip to my darlin skip to my lou

G7
Skip to my darlin' skip to my lou
C
Skip to my darlin skip to my lou
G7
Skip to my lou my darlin!
```

HE'S GOT THE WHOLE WORLD IN HIS HANDS

```
D
He's got the whole world in his hands
          A7
He's got the whole world in his hands
          D
He's got the whole world in his hands
      A7                    D
He's got the whole world in his hands.
```

DOWN IN THE VALLEY

```
A                          E7
Down in the valley, valley so low

                              A
Hear the wind blow love, hear the wind blow
```

THE DRUNKEN SAILOR

```
Am
What shall we do with the drunken sailor
G
What shall we do with the duunken sailor
Am
What shall we do with the drunken sailor
G           Am
Early in the morning.
```

SINNER MAN

```
Em
Oh sinner man where you goin' to run to?
D
Oh sinner man where you goin' to run to?
Em
Oh sinner man where you goin' to run to?
     D       Em
All on that day.
```

SKYE BOAT SONG

```
C                        G7
Speed bonny boat like a bird on the wing
C           F        C
Onward the sailors cry

                            G7
Carry the boy who was born to be king
C           F        C
Over the sea to Skye.

Am                       Dm
Loud the winds howl, loud the waves roar
Am
Thunderclaps rend the air;
C                    Dm
Baffled our foes stand by the shore
Am                       Am (G7)
Follow they will not dare
```

(repeat first four lines)

AMAZING GRACE

```
E                    A         E
Amazing grace how sweet the sound

                              B7
That saved a wretch like me
   E                    A         E
I once was lost but now am found
              B7
Was blind but now I see
```

MICHAEL ROW THE BOAT ASHORE

```
C
Michael row the boat ashore
                    F     C
Hal------le----lu------jah
Em                  Dm
Michael row the boat ashore
              C   G7    C
Hal------le----lu------jah
```

SCARBOROUGH FAIR

```
Am              G         Am
Are you going to Scarborough Fair
                    C    D   Am
Parsley, sage, rosemary and thyme
                C                G
Remember me to one who lived there
      Am    G              Am
For once he was a true love of mine.
```

The Complete Guitarist

"WERE I TO AWAIT PERFECTION MY BOOK WOULD NEVER BE FINISHED"
Tai T'ung, History of Chinese Writing (13th century)

First Edition: Summer 1974
Second Edition   Autumn 1974
Third Edition: Autumn 1975
Fourth Edition   Summer 1976

© Copyright   Michael Raven 1974

Book 2

Published by:

Stafford Spanish Guitar Centre

INTRODUCING TRIPLETS

(a)   The Quaver Triplet.   This is a triplet

A triplet is a group of three notes played in the time of two notes of the same value. They can be distinguished by a figure 3 and a curved line placed either underneath or above the group of three notes.   A triplet of quavers ♪♪♪ is equal to two quavers ♪♪   or one crotchet ♩

In practice it is often best to think of a quaver triplet as being equal to one crotchet, because that is usually the beat or count note.   Play the following exercises and keep a steady beat with your foot.   When you come to the triplets keep the beat going very firmly and on each beat count 1 2 3 ; or alternatively say the word 'Pel-i-can'.

Play slowly and deliberately

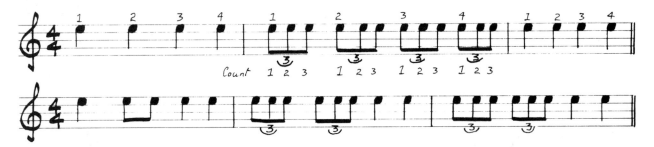

Play these exercises many times

(b)   The Crotchet Triplet

A triplet of crotchets ♩♩♩ is equal to two crotchets ♩♩   or one minim ♩
In practice it is often best to think of crotchet triplets as being equal to one minim. Below is an example of the crotchet triplet where the music is mainly four beats in the bar and the triplet is a divergence from the basic rhythm.   It will help you to play this correctly if you only beat two minims in the bar previous to the triplet.   The example makes this clear.

The tune Petite Fleur uses crotchet triplets. (turn to page 144)

Like so much in music these rhythms are not difficult to play, but can be confusing when written down.   This is where a good teacher can be of great service.   A simple demonstration in relation to the written symbol is worth many pages of verbal description.

BEAUTIFUL DREAMER

S. C. Foster arranged M. Raven

Milton at the age of Nineteen.

THE CADENCE

Introduction

The word cadence is derived from the Latin cado - "I fall". It is used to refer to either the fall of a melodic phrase to its final note, or the harmonisation of such a fall. We are concerned here with cadence harmonies.

Any harmonic progression (i.e., chord sequence) which suggests finality is technically a cadence. Some, however, are used far more than others. These are the Perfect Cadence The Plagal Cadence, and the Imperfect Cadence.

To fully understand the theory of cadences it is necessary to know something of scales and the chords based upon them. For ease of reference the required basic theory is outlined below.

Summary of Basic Theory

The most important notes in any scale (major, minor or modal) are named as follows:

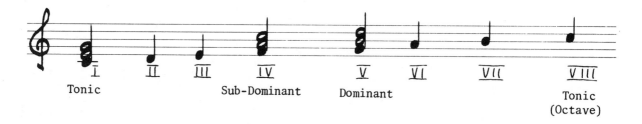

The chords based upon each note of the scale take the same name. The most important chords, or Primary Triads, are those based on the Root I, the Sub-Dominant IV, and the Dominant V. The notes of the primary triads can be duplicated and rearranged as the composer wishes.

The Cadences

The most common chord sequences that bring a piece of music to a conclusion are set out below using the scale and chords of C major as an example.

1.   The Perfect Cadence
     (American Authentic Cadence)

     The music is brought to a conclusion by moving from the Dominant V chord to the Tonic chord. This is the most common of all cadences, and is used to bring music to a final ending, or Full Close.

     Example:

2. The Plagal Cadence

The music is brought to a conclusion by moving from the Sub-Dominant to the Tonic.
The best known example of this cadence is the "Amen harmony" used in church music.
This is another example of the Full Close.

Example:

3. The Imperfect Cadence

The music is brought to a conclusion by moving from the Tonic to the Dominant. This
cadence does not normally conclude a piece finally, but rather one section, and is
therefore called a Half Close.

Example:

4. Interrupted Cadence
    (American Deceptive)

The music is brought to a conclusion by moving from the Dominant to any chord other
than the Tonic.   This cadence is used in much modern music.   One of the commonest
final chords is VI chord (A minor in the key of C major)

Example:

The four cadences described above were used by composers in the Baroque (1650 - 1750),
Classical (1750 - 1820), and Romantic (1820 -   ) periods.   In Renaissance times
(1500 - 1650) composers had not developed the major-minor tonality that we take for
granted today.   A piece of music would constantly change key, and is often described as
atonal - that is no fixed key or tonality.   (In recent years composers have reverted to
this idea, but in a much more extreme way, abandoning the notion of scales and keys
completely).

In keeping with the tonal flexibility of Renaissance music two somewhat unusual endings
were developed and extensively used.   These are the Phrygian Cadence and The Tierce de
Picardy.

The Phrygian Cadence

Music in a major key brought to a conclusion by ending on the Dominant chord of the
relative minor key.

Example:

The Tierce de Picardy   (The Flemish Third)

Music in a minor key is brought to a conclusion by ending on the major chord.   (A minor
chord consists of the Root, and a minor third and a perfect fifth above it.   A major
chord consists of the Root and a major third and a perfect fifth above it).   For example
music in the key of A minor would end with a chord of A major; music in the key of D
minor would end with a chord of D major.

This ending was very common in Renaissance times, but the origin of its name is unknown.

MODULATION

Very often a piece of music changes key.   This key change can be made in two ways.

(a)   It can be abrupt, the change being made without warning

(b)   It can modulate   from the old key to the new by means of an harmonic progression which prepares the ear for the new key and smooths over the transition.

The most commonly used modulation is very simple but extremely effective.   The new key is entered via its Dominant 7th (V7) chord.

Several of the pieces in this book modulate in just this fashion.   For example, "The Cossacka" by J. Kuffner on page 59 modulates from the key of E minor to the key of G major via the V7 chord (in this case D7) in bar 9, and back to E minor again by the V7 chord (in this case B7) in bar 13.

English Dance   M. Raven

Here is a short tune that modulates twice.   The first eight bars are in the key of C major.   The second section starts with a chord of E (with the seventh implied) which is used to modulate from C to the new key of A minor.   In bars 7 and 8 of this section a rather more subtle modulation occurs.   Though primarily a scale passage the implied harmony (i.e., chords) are D7 leading to G, leading to G7 which prepares the ear for a return to the key of C major.   Implied harmony is when the music makes the ear hear chords that are not actually sounded.   Play this piece through a few times and this idea will be made quite clear.

AN EXPLANATION OF TABLATURE NOTATION

Tablature or cifra as it is sometimes called, is a method of writing music for fretted instruments that avoids the abstract complexities of staff notation. It was developed and extensively used because it is much quicker to learn and easier to read than conventional notation. To this day lutenists read from tablature as a matter of course, including such virtuosos as Julian Bream. The lute and guitar music of such masters as Luis Milan, John Dowland and J.S. Bach was all first published in tablature and has only comparatively recently been transcribed into staff notation.

There were several kinds of tablature but that used today is a mixture of the Spanish and French systems.

Modern Guitar Tablature

Tablature is written on a 'stave' of six lines which represent the six strings of the guitar. The top line represents the 1st (thinnest) string and the bottom line the 6th (thickest) string. Numbers are placed on the lines to indicate at which fret the string is to be held down - thus:

0 means play the string open

1 means hold the string down behind the first fret

2 means hold the string down behind the second fret and so on

All musical symbols such as repeat signs, time signatures and the relative time values of notes are all identical to those used in staff notation. Only the notation of the longer notes differs. The semibreve and the minim are sometimes indicated by the lack of any sign, the context of the music making it clear what is required; and sometimes they are indicated by tied crotchets to the value required.

Au Clair de la lune

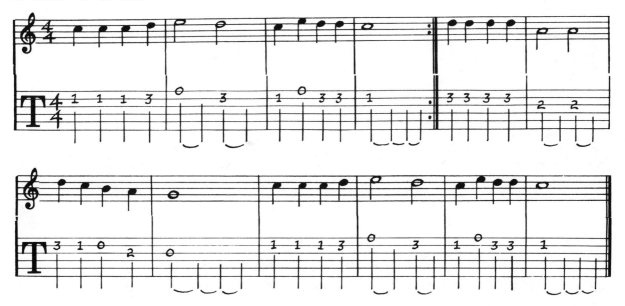

Lute music is written in a form of tablature identical in principle to that used for guitar music. The main difference is that the frets are identified by letter names instead of numerals. Thus a means open string, b means first fret, c means second fret, d means third fret, and so on.

Much lute music can be played on the guitar directly from lute tablature. To do this, however, necessitates retuning the 3rd (G) string of the guitar, which has to be lowered by one semitone to F sharp. The guitar is then in "lute" tuning.

LEARNING THE NATURAL NOTES ON THE FIRST STRING UP TO THE 12TH FRET

Introduction

The only new notes that we have to learn are the notes on the first string above the
fifth fret, but it is also necessary to learn some new alternative locations of notes we
already know.   To avoid confusion, the natural notes must be learned first and
thoroughly memorised.   This process may take many months and should not be rushed.
Once the natural notes are firmly established their sharps and flats are easily found.

Natural Notes on the First String up to the 12th fret

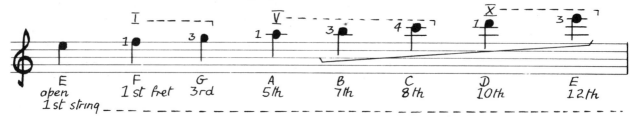

Once you have worked out the location of each note learn them thoroughly and practice
them daily.   Pay particular attention to the left hand fingering.   There are three
position changes.   Remember, Position is governed by the location of the index finger.
You should know the notes E F G and A (fifth fret), so practice especially the notes
from the seventh fret to the twelfth (enclosed by a bracket on the chart).

The twelfth fret on a standard Spanish guitar is located in line with the junction of
the guitar body and the neck.

Study in A minor   M. Raven

The purpose of this study is to give you practice in reading and locating the higher
notes on the first string.   Note the fingering very carefully.   The music consists of
four two bar phrases and each phrase is played in a different position.   The first
phrase for example is played with the index finger anchored at the fifth fret V.   In the
third bar the index finger moves up to the eighth fret VIII and the whole of the third
and fourth bars are played with the index finger anchored at that fret.   Do not remove
a finger until you absolutely have to.   In the first bar for example make the note A
with the first finger, then make the note B with the third finger but leave the first
finger in place; then make the note C with the fourth finger, but leaving the first
and third fingers in place on the finger board.   This procedure makes the location of
the notes much easier, and lets the notes flow smoothly one to the other - what is called
playing legato.   If the fingers are removed before playing the next note each note
sounds clipped and jerky - what is called staccato.

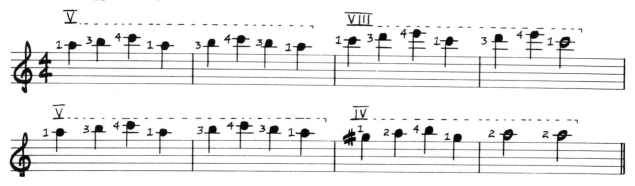

Lullaby

The melody is on the first string throughout.

M Raven

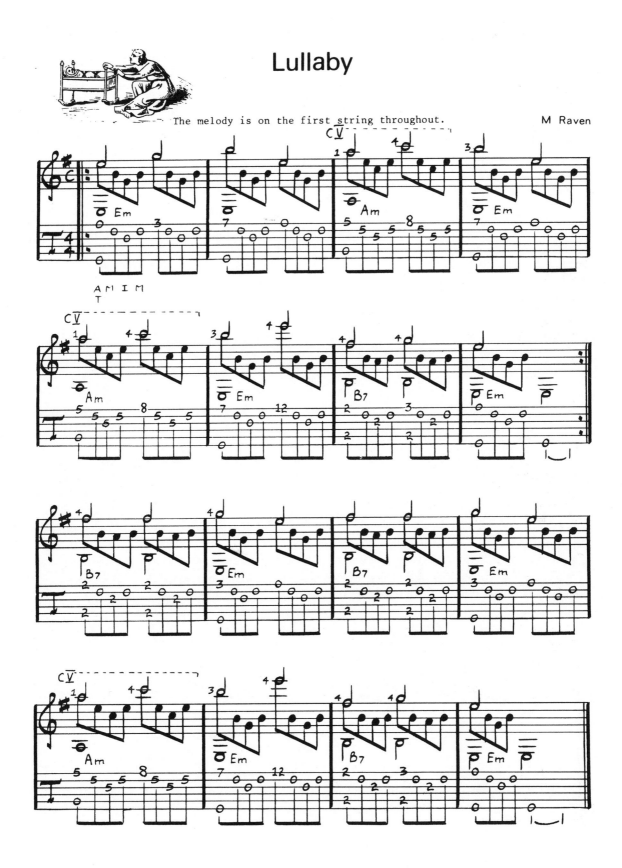

94

LEARNING THE NATURAL NOTES ON THE SECOND STRING UP TO THE 12TH FRET

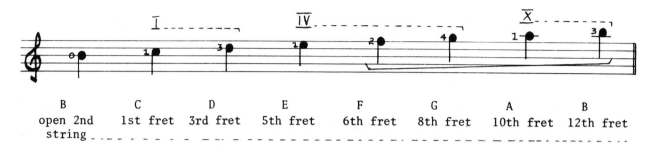

B	C	D	E	F	G	A	B
open 2nd string	1st fret	3rd fret	5th fret	6th fret	8th fret	10th fret	12th fret

Learn these notes, concentrating on the new notes (bracketed).   Then learn and practice
the following scale in thirds.   It will consolidate your knowledge of the new notes on
both the 1st and 2nd strings.   It is frequently used in solo guitar music and therefore
of great practical importance.   You will soon realise that the left hand fingers use two
shapes, thus:

(a) open   (b) closed

Scale in 3rds using natural notes on the 1st and 2nd strings

To give you time to think you can play each pair of notes 3 times thus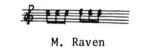

Camville

M. Raven

The index finger need never leave the seventh fret, 1st string.   It is anchored there
and makes the location of other notes easier.

COMPLETION OF THE FINGERBOARD

Learning the Natural Notes on the 6th string up to the 12th Fret

The reason for learning the notes on the 6th string at this stage is that like the 1st string the open 6th is tuned to a note of E.   This means that the same notes appear on the same fret, only they are two octaves lower.   You should therefore be able to name and play all the natural notes on the 6th string.   All that remains is to relate them to the stave.

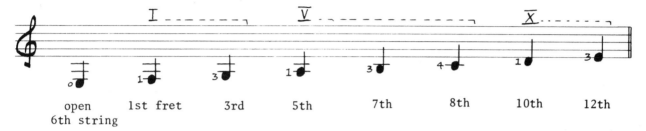

open   1st fret   3rd   5th   7th   8th   10th   12th
6th string

The learning of the notes on the 3rd and 4th and 5th strings should not be rushed.   A good idea is to learn one or two "guide notes" that enable you to calculate others in relation to them.   On the 3rd string the note of D at the 7th fret is a useful "guide note".   It is used a great deal in practice and is handily placed for calculating other notes above and below it.   Lastly, take your time on learning the notes on these last three strings.   It is not necessary to have learned these notes before going on to the next lessons, even though some of the pieces will necessitate the use of these notes.   You can always refer back to these pages when necessary.   Finally, remember that all the sharp and flat notes can be worked out from your knowledge of the natural notes.

Learning the Natural Notes on the 3rd string up to the 12th fret

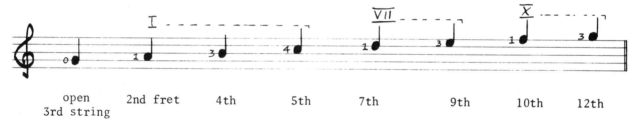

open   2nd fret   4th   5th   7th   9th   10th   12th
3rd string

Learning the Natural Notes on the 4th string up to the 12th fret

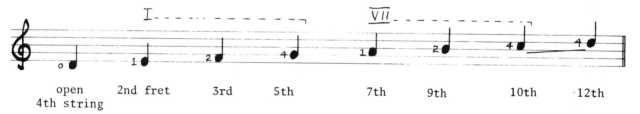

open   2nd fret   3rd   5th   7th   9th   10th   12th
4th string

Learning the Natural Notes on the 5th string up to the 12th fret

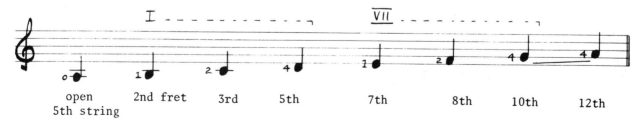

open   2nd fret   3rd   5th   7th   8th   10th   12th
5th string

On page four there is a chart of the complete fingerboard.

96

Mexican Waltz   Anonymous

C stands for cejilla which is the Spanish equivalent for barré

INTRODUCING THE OCTAVE SHAPE

A useful aid to learning the notes made at the higher frets is the "Octave Shape".   This
is a "trick of the trade" that for some reason rarely finds its way in to tutors.   The
player must first learn the notes on the 1st and 2nd strings.   By using octave shapes he
can then work out quite easily the names of the notes on the other four strings at all
positions.

  1. The octave shape linking the 1st and 3rd strings

If the first string is held down at a particular fret, then a note of the same name (but
sounding an octave lower) is made by holding down the 3rd string three frets lower, thus:

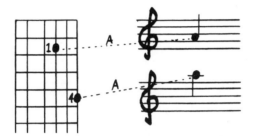

This relationship is constant.   Move the shape one fret, thus:

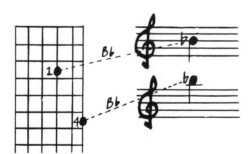

and the note of B♭ on the 1st string is echoed on the 3rd string, only an octave lower.

  2.   The octave shape linking the 1st and 4th strings

  A similar shape exists linking the 1st and 4th strings thus:

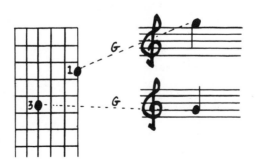

98

3. The octave shape linking the 2nd and 5th strings

The same shape as in 2 transferred one string towards the bass links the notes found on the 2nd and 5th strings, thus:

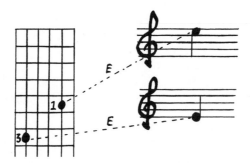

4. The octave shape linking the 1st and 6th strings

The relationship of the notes on the 1st string to the 6th string has already been mentioned. The same notes occur at the same frets, but two octaves apart, thus:

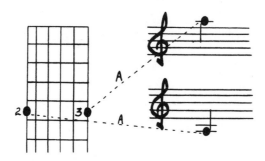

Finally, these octave shapes are of more than theoretical value. They are used a great deal in all kinds of guitar music. Flamenco and jazz guitarists in particular find them of the greatest value. Wes Montgomery who was probably the leading jazz guitarist in the world before his recent death was particularly fond of octave playing, so much so that it became a very distinctive part of his style. He would play a melody and accompany it with notes an octave below, which is easy to do because the same shape is kept throughout. Flamenco guitarists use octave shapes in exactly the same way.

CLASSIFICATION OF TIME SIGNATURES

Time signatures can be classified in two ways:

1) by the number of beats to the bar that they indicate

    a) Duple time   =   two beats to the bar
    b) Triple time   =   three beats to the bar
    c) Quadruple time =   four beats to the bar

2) by the number by which the beat (not the number of beats) is most easily divisible

    a) Simple time   =   the beat note is divisible by 2
    b) Compound time =   the beat note is divisible by 3

    For example, four-four time is simple, one beat (a crotchet) divides most easily into two quavers ♩ = ♫ whereas six-eight time is compound, one beat (a dotted crotchet) divides most easily into three quavers ♩· = ♫♪

Bouree (a fairly fast old French dance)   Anon.

Grade II group A Trinity College

99

THE MODES

Since the time of J.S. Bach the composers of most serious and popular music have restricted themselves to just two of the seven scales or Modes available.   The favoured two are the Ionian (what we call the Major scale) and the Aeolian (what we call the ancient Minor scale).   The remaining five, the Dorian, Phrygian, Lydian, Mixolydian and Locrian have been largely ignored.

However, with the current interest in folk music, flamenco and modern jazz has come a renewed interest in these little known scales.   Many of the most beautiful of British folk melodies are in the Dorian and Mixolydian modes; flamenco songs and guitar music owe much of their distinctive character to the fact that they use the Phrygian mode; and exponents of modern jazz are exploring all the modes in a search for new sounds.

So what are the Modes?   A mode is simply a scale.   It is the order of tones and semi-tones that makes one mode different from another.   This should be easy to understand because we are already familiar with two of the modes - the Ionian (Major Scale) and the Aeolian (Minor Scale).   To refresh your memory here are the tone-semitone orders of these two scales:

Ionian
(Major Scale):   tone   tone   semitone   tone   tone   tone   semitone

Aeolian
(Minor Scale):   tone   semitone   tone   tone   semitone tone   tone

The easiest way to construct the modes is to use only the natural notes and build a scale on each note.   If no sharps or flats are used then the Tone - Semitone order will be different each time, and all the modes will have been constructed.

The Modes (using only the Natural Notes)

```
Ionian Mode (C to C)        C   D   E   F   G   A   B   C
                              t   t   s   t   t   t   s
Dorian Mode (D to D)            D   E   F   G   A   B   C   D
                                  t   s   t   t   t   s   t
Phrygian Mode (E to E)              E   F   G   A   B   C   D   E
                                      s   t   t   t   s   t   t
Lydian Mode (F to F)                    F   G   A   B   C   D   E   F
                                          t   t   t   s   t   t   s
Mixolydian Mode (G to G)                    G   A   B   C   D   E   F   G
                                              t   t   s   t   t   s   t
Aeolian Mode (A to A)                           A   B   C   D   E   F   G   A
                                                  t   s   t   t   s   t   t
Locrian Mode (B to B)                               B   C   D   E   F   G   A   B
                                                      s   t   t   s   t   t   t
```

Just as the major scale can exist in many different keys by using sharps and flats to maintain the correct major scale order of tones and semitones, so can all the other modes. This might make it difficult for you to do work out the mode of a particular tune, but all you have to do is write out the scale used in the melody, calculate the order of tones and semitones and then refer to the chart above.

For example the scale   A B C D E F# G A
has a tone semitone order of   t s t t t s t

Looking at the chart above we see that this scale is in the Dorian mode.   As its keynote is A we can say that a melody based on this scale is in the key of A Dorian mode.

I'll go Enlist for a Sailor (key D, Dorian mode)   English Trad.

The Handsome Cabin Boy (key G, Mixolydian mode)   English Trad.

TRANSPOSING CHORDS

To transpose the chords of a song from one key to another follow this procedure

Write out the notes of original scale - the old key, and underneath write out the notes of the scale to which you wish to transpose the chords - the new key. As an example we will transpose a chord sequence from the key of C major to the key of G major.

	Scale of C Major							
Old Key	C	D	E	F	G	A	B	C

	Scale of G Major							
New Key	G	A	B	C	D	E	F#	G

Remember, chords are built on scales. If we transpose the notes of the scale, we transpose their chords with them. The note of C in the old scale is equivalent to the note G in the new scale. Likewise are the chords based on them. Wherever we had the chord of C we now have the chord of G. The chord of G7 in the key of C major becomes the chord of D7 in the key of G major. It is as simple as that. Any qualification of a chord - such as 7, min 7, aug, etc., is simply transposed with it. Here is an example:

Chord sequence in the key of C major is C Am Dm G7 C (old). Transposing by means of the comparative scales above we see that C becomes G and Am becomes Em, etc. So the same chord sequence in the key of G major is G Em Am D7 G (new).

Chord sequences in minor keys can be transposed in exactly the same way. Simply write out the letter names of the two scales and proceed as above.

102

Allemande (means "German dance")

Anon.

Grade III group A Trinity College

Andante (means "at a moderate tempo")   F. Sor

Grade III group B Trinity College

KEYS AND KEY SIGNATURES

The most important reason for having more than one key is purely and simply that we often need to sing or play the same music at different pitches.   A young boy will sing a melody at a higher pitch than a grown man.   The young boy has a high voice and therefore sings in a high key; a man has a low voice and therefore sings in a low key.   The only difference between keys is one of pitch.   A major scale is a major scale regardless of its pitch.   However, if a major scale is built on any note other than the note C then one or more of the natural notes will have to be altered - i.e., sharpened or flattened, to maintain the correct tone - semitone order.

These altered notes constitute what we call the Key Signature.   The Key Signature could be determined by a process of trial and error but it is more satisfactory if we can discern some logical method by which the altered notes of each key can be determined. There are, in fact, two procedures for determining the Key Signatures of scales at different pitches - one for the "sharp keys" and one for the "flat keys".

Procedure for Deducing the Key Signatures of the Sharp Keys.

If we build a new scale on the fifth note of the scale of C major we have to sharpen the leading note (i.e., the 7th note) of the new scale to maintain the correct tone - semitone order of the Major scale.   Thus:

```
1 2 3 4 5 6 7 8
C D E F G A B C
        G A B C D E F# G
        1 2 3 4 5 6 7  8
```

The key signature of the scale of G major is therefore

If we continue this procedure, starting a new scale on the fifth note of the old scale and sharpening the 7th note of the new scale, all the "sharp keys" can be deduced.

Procedure for Deducing the Key Signatures of the Flat Keys

If we build a new scale on the fourth note of the scale of C major we have to flatten the fourth note of the new scale to maintain the correct tone - semitone order of the major scale.   Thus:

```
1 2 3 4 5 6 7 8
C D E F G A B C
      F G A Bb C D E F
      1 2 3 4  5 6 7 8
```

The key signature of the F major scale is therefore

If we continue this procedure, starting a new scale on the fourth note of the old and flattening the fourth note of the new scale, all the "flat keys" can be deduced.

The Key Signatures of Minor Scales

It is not necessary to work out the key signatures for the minor keys.   All we have to do
is remember that each major key has a related minor key which shares the same key
signature.   Minor keys have the same name as the sixth note of their related major keys -
e.g.,

1. Scale of C major

```
1 2 3 4 5 6 7 8
C D E F G A B C
```

A minor is the relative minor of C major.

2. Scale of G major

```
1 2 3 4 5 6 7 8
G A B C D E F#G
```

E minor is the relative minor of G major

3. Scale of D major

```
1 2 3  4 5 6 7  8
D E F# G A B C# D
```

What is the relative minor of D major?

Here is a complete table of all major and minor key signatures.

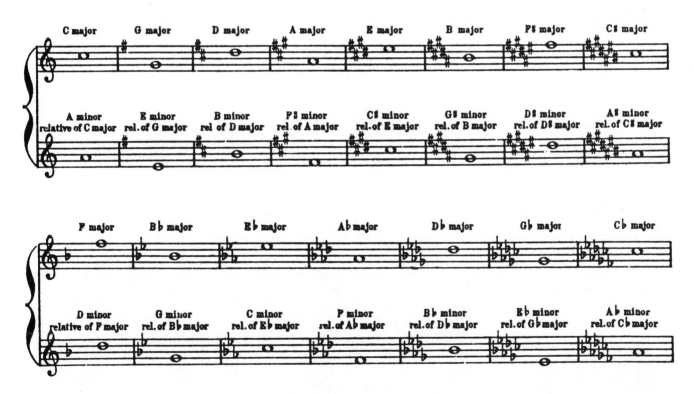

THEORY OF INTERVALS PART II

In an earlier lesson we discussed the basic theory of intervals. There is, however, a little more to be said on this subject. In particular we must look at the detailed naming of the basic intervals and their altered variants.

We have seen that an interval is the distance between two sounds and consists of an upper note and a lower note. The size of an interval may be calculated by counting the letter names upwards, from the lower note to the higher note, both notes being included in the total. The interval from C to D for example, contains two letter names and is therefore a second; that from C to E contains three letter names, and is therefore a third, and so on.

The sharpening or flattening of either or both the notes forming an interval does not alter its numerical name; thus the intervals C flat to D, C to D, and C sharp to D are all seconds though each differs in quality. We must now learn the four important rules that govern the quality of an interval.

RULE 1

ANY INTERVAL WHICH IS COUNTED FROM THE FIRST NOTE OF A MAJOR SCALE TO ANY OTHER NOTE OF THAT SCALE IS EITHER A PERFECT OR A MAJOR INTERVAL.

Major 2nd	Major 3rd	Perfect 4th	Perfect 5th	Major 6th	Major 7th	(Octave) Perfect 8th

Rule 2

If a major interval, (a second, third, sixth or seventh) is reduced by a semitone either by flattening the upper note or sharpening the lower note, it becomes a minor interval.

Rule 3

If a perfect or a major interval is increased by a semitone either by sharpening the upper note or flattening the lower note, it becomes an augmented interval.

Rule 4

If a perfect or a minor interval is reduced by a semitone, either by flattening the upper note or by sharpening the lower note, it becomes a diminished interval.

Charlie Byrd

Django Reinhardt

Sabicas

Interval		No. of Semitones
unison	C - C	0
Diminished Second	C - Dbb	0
Minor Second	C - Db	1
Major Second	C - D	2
Augmented Second	C - D#	3
Diminished Third	C - Ebb	2
Minor Third	C - Eb	3
Major Third	C - E	4
Augmented Third	C - E#	5
Diminished Fourth	C - Fb	4
Perfect Fourth	C - F	5
Augmented Fourth	C - F#	6
Diminished Fifth	C - Gb	6
Perfect Fifth	C - G	7
Augmented Fifth	C - G#	8
Diminished Sixth	C - Abb	7
Minor Sixth	C - Ab	8
Major Sixth	C - A	9
Augmented Sixth	C - A#	10
Diminished Seventh	C - Bbb	9
Minor Seventh	C - Bb	10
Major Seventh	C - B	11
Augmented Seventh	C - B#	12
Diminished Eighth	C - Cb	11
Perfect Eighth (octave)	C - C	12
Augmented Eighth	C - C#	13

A better understanding of how the more obstruse (and little used) intervals are named will be obtained by studying the following example.

    C - Ebb   =   a diminished Third   (2 semitones)
    C - D   =   a Major Second   (2 semitones)

1. C - Ebb   is called a Third because the interval contains three letter names C D E

2. C - D   is called a Second because the interval contains only two letter names C D

3. Remember, a double flat (bb) lowers a note by two semitones. Double flat notes are always enharmonics of the preceding natural note and for the most part are only of theoretical interest.   Ebb is the enharmonic of D; on tempered scale instruments, such as the guitar and piano, these two notes are identical.   This will be made clearer by writing out the chromatic scale of C major including the enharmonics of the natural notes, thus:

C	C#	D	D#	E	F	F#	G	G#	A	A#	B
B#	Db	Ebb	Eb	Fb	E#	Gb	Abb	Ab	Bbb	Bb	Cb
Dbb	BX	CX	Fbb	DX	Gbb	EX	FX		GX	Cbb	AX

(The sign for a double sharp is an 'X')

RULE FOR NAMING THE QUALITY OF ANY INTERVAL

In music theory examinations candidates are often asked to fully describe the name and quality of a number of intervals. No key signature is given in such test examples, as none indeed is necessary. The rule to follow in working such examples is as follows.

IMAGINE THE LOWER NOTE OF THE INTERVAL TO BE THE ROOT NOTE OF THE MAJOR SCALE OF THE SAME NAME. If the higher note of the interval belongs to this scale then it must be either perfect or major (all 4ths, 5ths and octaves are perfect; all 2nds, 3rds, 6ths and 7ths are major). For example, if the higher note is six letter names above the lower root note it must be a <u>major</u> 6th, if it is five letter names away it must be a <u>perfect</u> 5th. If, however, the higher note does not belong to the major scale based on the lower note the interval must be either greater or smaller than a perfect or major interval. The rules governing the naming of such intervals have already been given. Note that this method of naming intervals depends upon you knowing, or being able to work out, the key signatures (the sharps and flats) of every key. Here are some examples:

Example 1

Question: Describe fully the interval between these two notes

Reasoning: Taking C as the root note of a major scale (C major) we see that the note B belongs to the scale. There are seven note names in the interval; it is therefore a 7th. All the intervals from the root note of a major scale are either perfect or major. Only 4ths, 5ths and octaves are perfect, therefore the interval is a major 7th.

Answer: The interval C to B is a major 7th.

Example 2

Question: Fully describe the interval between these two notes

Reasoning: Taking C as the root note of a major scale (C major) we see that the note G sharp does not belong to this scale. The interval from C to G is a 5th, and if the note had not been sharpened it would have been a perfect 5th. But it has been sharpened and when a perfect interval is increased by a semitone it is said to be augmented.

Answer: The interval C to G sharp is an augmented 5th.

Example 3

Question: Describe fully the interval between these two notes

Reasoning: Make G the root note of a major scale, that is G major. The interval between the notes G and B is a major third. (Remember the rule: all intervals from the root note of a major scale are either perfect or major - all 4ths, 5ths and octaves are perfect; all other intervals are major). However, the higher note is not B, but B flat. When a major interval is reduced by a semitone it becomes minor.

Answer: The interval G to B flat is a minor third.

Barcarole

Napoleon Coste

Grade III group B Trinity College
Barcarole means "boating song", especially of the kind sung by Venetian gondoliers.

moderator cantabile (cantabile means song-like, play expressively).

TONE PRODUCTION - LEFT HAND TECHNIQUES

One of the trade marks of a good player is the quality, control and variety of the tone
he produces.   Tonal variety can be achieved by the application of several techniques.
In this lesson those techniques involving the left hand will be described, but the
student must be fully aware that in this all important field of study, a good teacher
can be of the utmost assistance.   The serious student should also make a point of
listening carefully to recordings of good players.

The technique of Vibrato

When the left hand finger that holds a string to the fret board is moved very quickly
from side to side after the note has been plucked, the effect is to very slightly alter
the pitch of the note.   This small but rapid alteration of pitch is called vibrato.
There are two ways of producing vibrato.

(a)   The string can be pulled and pushed from side to side, to and from the player as
      shown in the diagram.

      Care has to be taken when using this side to side movement that it is not done
      excessively or the note will be distorted to the point where it "wails", a sound
      which is most effective in blues and rock but out of place in classical music.

(b)   Vibrato can also be produced by rocking the left hand finger up and down in a line
      parallel with the string.

      This is the vibrato technique used by other stringed instrument players such as
      violinists and cellists.   It is more difficult than the first technique but is
      particularly useful on the first string where the use of the side to side movement
      involves the risk of pushing the string over the edge of the fretboard.

The quality of the vibrato achieved by both methods can be varied by altering the
rapidity and degree of the movement.   More than any other one technique the quality and
use of vibrato gives a player his own distinctive "sound".   Finally it should be pointed
out that the use of vibrato is not reserved just for single note passages, but can be
used on several notes at the same time.   It is even possible to use it on six string
chords, in which case the whole hand "shakes" using either the "side to side" or "up and
down" movements.

Ligado

The technique of ligado, that is hammering on and pulling off, was discussed in an
earlier lesson.   It is only mentioned here for the sake of completeness.

The Slide

The third important left hand technique is the slide of which there are two varieties known as Portamento and Glissando.

(a) Portamento

Portamento literally means "carrying" one note to the other. It is a term that was originally applied to singing and was extensively used in Non-conformist hymn singing in the nineteenth century. It refers to the scooping sound obtained by sliding from one note to the next sounding all the intermediary notes.

This sound is imitated on the guitar by playing a note and then sliding the same finger to the next note without reducing the pressure, thus sounding all the intervening notes. Study this example, and note the fingering:

written   played

Note: A right hand finger usually plucks the second note, but not always.

The portamento is not usually marked in the music except by implication of the fingering It is an effect that is largely left to the discretion of the player. It is widely used in slow expressive music of the Romantic period.

(b) The Glissando

The glissando is performed in the same way as portamento. It is distinguished from portamento on three counts; first, the interval between the two notes is usually much larger; second, the intervening notes are made to sound more distinctly, like a very fast scale passage; and third, it is marked in the music by a line joining the two notes, and sometimes by the abbreviation "gliss", or in folk blues music "slide".

written   or

Note: A right hand finger usually plucks the second note, but not always.

TONE PRODUCTION - RIGHT HAND TECHNIQUES

1. Care of Nails

Probably the most important factor in tone production is the condition of the right hand nails. They should protrude about one sixteenth of an inch beyond the tip of the finger, judged with the palm facing you. If the nails are too long speed is impaired because they tend to "stick" on the strings and produce a rather weak, thin tone. If too short they make control of the stroke difficult and tend to catch irregularly - some times the nails catch the string, sometimes not. The nails should be polished with very fine emery cloth after filing, especially the inside edge which makes contact with the string. If this is not done it takes four or five hours of playing before the sharp scratchy edge is smoothed off by contact with the strings.

2. Apoyando and Tirando

The techniques of Apoyando (the rest stroke) and Tirando (the free stroke) were discussed in the first lessons. Here it must be mentioned that the two strokes produce different sounds. A note played with the free stroke sounds bright and clean cut; a note played with the rest stroke sounds fuller and richer. Where the music allows of a choice of stroke be aware of the tonal difference and select the most fitting.

3. Metallico and Dolce

Tonal contrast can also be obtained by either plucking the strings near the bridge, which produces a hard metallic sound, or near the fretboard which produces a soft sweet (dolce = sweet) sound. Metallico is sometimes indicated by the phrase sul ponticello, literally "on the bridge". Generally speaking the free stroke is used when playing near the bridge to add to the harsher brighter sound; and the rest stroke when playing near the fretboard.

Practice this example

metallico (use free stroke)   dolce (use rest stroke)

4. Legato and Staccato

(a) Legato

Most melodies should be played legato, that is in a smooth and flowing fashion, as if sung. When playing a slow melody many beginners make the mistake of bringing the plucking finger into contact with the string in anticipation. The effect is to damp the note and cause small breaks in the continuity of sound. The right hand plucking fingers must be held back till the last possible moment and then come down sufficiently quickly to avoid a break in the flow of sound. It should be noted that all the left hand techniques discussed in the last lesson are also aids to legato playing.

(b) Staccato

The opposite of legato is staccato. The notes are played crisply and damped immediately after being sounded. Notes to be played staccato are marked with a dot placed beneath the symbol thus: ♪ This means in effect that the note is halved in value, and the lost time made up for by a period of silence.

Example:

written   played

When a note is marked thus ♪ it means that it should be played even more staccato, that is, as clipped as possible. The actual techniques used to stop the notes sustaining are those described in the discussion of Rest Signs in an earlier lesson. To sum up briefly, a note can be damped by (a) releasing the left hand pressure, (b) by placing a right hand plucking finger on the string thus stopping it from vibrating, and (c) by a combination of both these techniques.

2}

HARMONICS

Any note produced by an instrument is accompanied by a varying number of secondary notes called harmonics, or overtones. The vibration of the string as a whole produces the fundamental note, and secondary vibrations within the string length produce the harmonics For example the note C is caused by a string vibrating and creating in the air wavelengths of a certain frequency and the harmonics (C an octave higher, the G above that, the C above that, the E above that and so on) are caused by smaller wavelengths superimposed on the main wavelength.

This is not an exact explanation, in fact the phenomenon is still being researched, but is sufficiently accurate for practical purposes.

By lightly touching a string at certain points, the fundamental wavelength can be restrained and only the secondary wavelengths be allowed to continue. Thus the fundamental note is held in abeyance and only the harmonics allowed to sound.

Technique of making Natural Harmonics on the Guitar

1. Lightly touch the 6th string with the third finger above the twelfth fret. Not behind the fret but actually above the fret wire itself. Do not press the string on to the fret, but just touch it lightly.

2. Pluck the string with the right hand thumb. Play forcefully and slightly nearer the bridge than usual.

3. Immediately after having plucked the string remove the left hand finger. The actions of plucking and removal of the left hand finger are almost instantaneous.

The resulting sound should be a bell-like tone an octave above the E of the open string. If you do not succeed at your first attempt, then persevere, it is not at all difficult. Repeat the procedure on the other five strings.

Harmonics can also be produced at the seventh fret and the fifth fret, though at these positions they are appreciably weaker, and even at the fourth fret where they are weaker still.

Harmonics are often represented by diamond shaped notes and/or the abbreviation harm. or arm. from armonico. The actual pitch of the harmonic is sometimes written or alternatively the pitch of the open string with a numeral to say at which fret it should be touched. Here are the natural harmonics of all six strings. They are written an octave lower than the actual sound to avoid excessive use of leger lines.

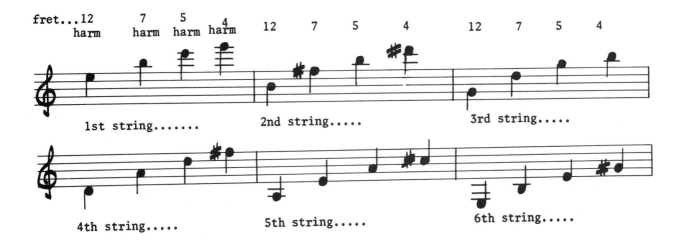

It is interesting to note that the natural harmonics of an open string make a major triad. The harmonics of the 1st string, for example, make a chord of E major, the 2nd string B major, and so on.

Artificial or Octave Harmonics

We have seen by experiment that the harmonic produced at the twelfth fret has the strongest sound. The twelfth fret divides the open string into two equal halves and the note made at that fret is an octave above the open string. Suppose now that we hold down the 1st string behind the first fret. To halve the length of the string we must now go to the thirteenth fret. Stop the string at the second fret, and the octave will be found at the fourteenth fret, and so on.

fret 0 - 12, 1 - 13. 2 - 14, 3 - 15, 4 - 16, etc.

To make artificial harmonics we utilise this fact by touching a string with the first finger of the right hand at a distance of twelve frets above the note held down by the left hand. The string is then plucked by the ring (a) finger of the right hand, as shown in the photograph.

Here is an example of artificial harmonics.

To play the example, follow this procedure:

1. Make the note F on the 1st string at the first fret.

2. Lightly touch the string with the right hand index (i) finger at the thirteenth fret (twelve frets above the note being held).

3. Pluck the string with the third finger (a) of the right hand whilst the index (i) finger maintains contact. Remove the index finger immediately after plucking the string.

4. Make the note G with the left hand, third (3) finger.

5. Lightly touch the string with the right hand index (i) finger at the fifteenth fret (twelve frets above the note being held).

6. Pluck the string with the third (a) finger of the right hand and remove the index (i) finger immediately after plucking the string.

7. Make the note F and repeat the procedure of 2 and 3 above.

Harmonics with Chords

As it is only necessary to use the index and ring fingers to make octave harmonics the middle finger and thumb of the right hand can play other strings so making a chord with a harmonic as its top note.

Example:

To play this example: 1) make the chord with the left hand, 2) lightly touch the 1st string above the twelfth fret with the index finger of the right hand and pluck the string with the ring finger, 3) pluck the 3rd string with the middle finger and the 5th string with the thumb. All pluck simultaneously of course.

Cuckoo Waltz   Anonymous

Right hand position for making artificial (octave) harmonics

116

THE TREMOLO

Unlike such instruments as the violin, the flute and the organ, the acoustic Spanish
guitar cannot sustain a note for any length of time. Almost immediately after a
string has been plucked the note it produces dies away. All solo guitar music
depends on this fact, for if every note rang out until deliberately stopped most of
our music would become something of a shambles with unwanted sounds lingering on.
One has only to try playing classical music on an electric guitar with the controls
set for maximum sustain (as in much rock music) to get some idea of the effect. It
can sound pretty awful.

There are occasions however when we want to sustain melody notes, especially when they
are of long duration. Modern recording studio techniques provide several solutions
and are widely used when the classical guitar is used in popular music. The most
common method is to use artificial echo, the rapid repeating of a note having the effect
of sustaining it. (Concert guitarists do in fact adjust the tempo of the pieces they
play to suit the acoustics of a particular hall. The more echo there is the more
slowly a piece should be played. Indeed a fast piece - a jig or a bourree for example -
should not be played too quickly in a hall with a lot of echo because the notes tend to
blur together).

However, there is another method of sustaining melody notes on the guitar - or rather a
technique that imitates the effect. It is called Tremolo, and is one of the most
impressive sounds that can be conjured from a guitar. Before describing this technique
the student should be warned that the majority of players find the tremolo difficult,
including some professional concert artists. This is reflected in the fact that very
few pieces using this technique have been written for the guitar - classical composers
like their music to be played and are very conscious of not making things unnecessarily
difficult. Flamenco guitarists on the other hand are brought up to accept that they
have to develop a reasonable tremolo because it forms an integral part of modern technique.

Tremolo can be produced by one of several slightly different techniques, the most
important of which is the basic classical tremolo.

a) Classical Tremolo

The thumb plays an accompaniment note and the melody note is played three times by the
ring, middle and index fingers in that order.

Example:

To save space the tremolo is sometimes written thus:

The thumb and fingers all play free strokes.   The fingers must use the minimum of movement to avoid catching adjacent strings.

To be effective the tremolo must be played reasonably quickly.   The faster it is executed the more individual notes will blur into one another giving the effect of a continuous sound.   To attain speed play very slowly at first so that the hand learns the correct action thoroughly.   Then slowly increase the speed, but be certain that the notes are still being played evenly and in the correct order.   Do not try for great speed too early.

When practising the tremolo it is often helpful to over-emphasise the strokes of the fingers.   Deliberately pluck very hard and therefore loudly.   Play a few bars in this way, and then revert to a normal strength of plucking and volume level.   You should find that the second time you can play quite a lot more quickly and fluently. The best way to practice tremolo is to hold nut position chords and tremolo the first string whilst the thumb plays a pattern such as that shown in the example.   When you have achieved some degree of success on the first string try to tremolo on the second and third strings.   This is considerably more difficult.

b)   The Flamenco Tremolo

The flamenco tremolo differs from the Classical in that it includes an extra note.

As can be seen from the example the extra note is played by the index finger.   The flamenco tremolo was developed because flamenco guitarists often have to play at a fixed tempo when they are accompanying dancers and singers, and this tempo is often too slow for the Classical tremolo to be effective.   So to play at a slowish tempo and still maintain continuity in the melody an extra note was inserted.

c)   Two-Finger Tremolo

When a flamenco guitarist wants a very fast strong tremolo sound then he uses the two finger tremolo.   This differs from the orthodox techniques in that the finger and thumb pluck together.   It is normally executed with thumb, index and middle fingers, thus:

To obtain an even stronger louder sound the fingers can play apoyando.   This tremolo is quite easy to perform and can be used as an alternative to the Classical tremolo - but it does not have the same smooth flow of sound at slower speeds.

Finally, it should be mentioned that the tremolo is sometimes used on a drone note, the melody being played by the thumb; and also that on some occasions a flamenco guitarist will often deliberately tremolo two (or even three) strings together, giving the effect of a chordal tremolo, though this is never indicated in the music.

Pizzicato (Etouffe)

This is the term used to indicate that the strings of instruments which are normally
bowed, should be plucked with the fingers.   The sound produced could be described as
a muffled staccato.   On the guitar we can imitate this sound by plucking a string
with the side of the right hand thumb whilst the side of the right hand damps on
strings close to the bridge.   Pizzicato is indicated in music by the word
Pizzicato, or the abbreviation pizz.

Right hand position for playing pizzicato

The Tabour

A wide variety of drum effects can be obtained from the guitar by tapping the front,
back and sides in various ways.   The most common is to tap the strings with either the
sides of the thumb or the flat of the middle finger on or very close to the bridge.
This produces a heavy drum-like sound through which can be heard the resonance of the
strings.

The Snare Drum

A very startling effect can be obtained by crossing the 5th string over the 6th string
at a high fret - say the ninth.   The two strings are crossed and held to the finger
board; when struck they produce a sound remarkably like that of a snare drum.   It is
possible to hold the crossed strings with the left hand index finger and use the
remaining fingers to hold notes on the remaining four strings.   This is done in the
flamenco Saeta and the author's "Lichfield Greenhill Bower Processional".   In both
these examples the remaining fingers hold the notes of a chord which are plucked so as
to imitate a bugle call (all bugle calls are based on the three notes of a major triad).

Golpe

Golpe is a term used in flamenco to indicate the tapping of the sound board by either
the fingers or thumb.   Such taps are used (a) to fill missing beats in a syncopated
melody, and (b) to accent a main beat note.   The tap (or Golpe) is indicated
variously by a letter G, a box □ or a cross ✕ .   Remember, flamenco guitars have
plastic sheets (called golpeadores) to protect the wood from the finger nails.

ORNAMENTATION

A piece of music can be decorated with musical embellishments called ornaments. Some times these are marked but more often they are left to the discretion of the performer. Ornamentation is not as important today as it was in other musical periods, such as the Renaissance, but nevertheless some knowledge of this subject is required if the performer wishes to play ancient music with any degree of authenticity.

The Mordent

Today the mordent is more usually written as in example (b) because there is then no ambiguity as to whether the lower note should be a tone or a semitone below the main note.

If a bass note is written below the main note it is not played with the main note, but with the first note of the ornament. The ornament does in fact borrow time from the main note, for example:

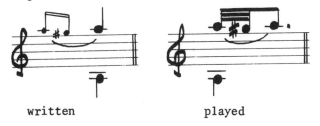

Note the slur sign which indicates that only the first A is plucked, the G sharp is made by pulling-off, and the A for the second time by hammering-on.

The mordent was used extensively in Renaissance and Baroque music. In later periods and especially in music of Spanish origin, the Reverse Mordent was favoured.

The Reverse Mordent

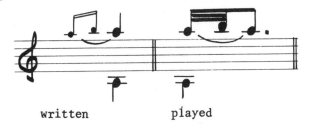

The musical example is self-explanatory, but once again remember that if a bass note is written beneath the main note it is played with the first note of the ornament.

120

The Turn

written   played

The inverted S sign indicates the note over which it is placed should be played thus
(a) play the note of the scale above the main note, (b) play the main note itself,
(c) play the note of the scale below the main note, (d) play the main note itself.
These four notes are to be played in the time of the indicated value of the main note.
Pulling-off and hammering-on are used wherever possible.

The Trill

(a) The Baroque Trill

written   played

The Trill starts on the note of the scale above the main note as shown in the example.
On the guitar the trill is usually executed using hammering on and pulling off, only
the first note actually being plucked.

It was not uncommon to end a trill with a turn especially if a note of long value
preceded the final chord.   For example:

written   played

(b) The Classical Trill

written   played

The Classical Trill commences with the main note itself and is rapidly alternated with
the note of the scale above it.   The exact number of notes is left to the performer
and is usually quite simply how many he can fit into the given note value, in this case
a crotchet.

The Acciaccatura

This was fully discussed in an earlier lesson, and it is only necessary to add that this ornament is occasionally referred to somewhat confusingly as a fast Appoggiatura.

The Appoggiatura

Sometimes called the slow appoggiatura, the small note borrows half the value of the succeeding note.   In modern music printing this ornament is not normally indicated it being less confusing to write the notes as played.

Example:

written   played

The Rolled Chord

Normally the notes of a chord are sounded together but a pleasing effect can be obtained by plucking the strings one after the other in the form of a fast arpeggio. The notes ripple or roll one after the other.   To perform this roll place the thumb on a bass string and the three fingers on the treble strings.   Pluck first with the thumb and then quickly and evenly with one finger after the other.   The roll is indicated by a wavy line placed next to the chord.

Study this example:

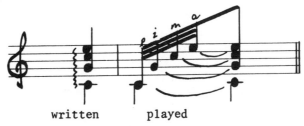

written   played

The rolled chord is particularly effective in music played at a slow tempo.   The separation of the notes helps to sustain the sound and softens the attack of the fingers on the strings.   The roll is an established part of lute technique, for the lute has even less volume and sustain than the guitar.

To play a six note chord the thumb plucks the three bass strings, the fingers the treble strings in the usual way, thus:

written   played

Sometimes, the rolled chord is played entirely by the thumb, which sweeps across all the strings.   This is indicated in the music by a wavy line with p for pulgar (thumb) written next to it.   This is a great deal easier to perform and the student should avoid the temptation to use this method as a substitute for the thumb-fingers technique.   The thumb roll is usually only used either at the end of a section of the music to suggest a bold, rich finality, or to provide a broken chord accompaniment to a free rhythm song.

INTERPRETATION

The notes of a piece of music are, as it were, a musical skeleton which requires clothing with flesh and blood by the performer.   A suitable tempo must be chosen; the volume levels varied and the tone altered from passage to passage; the rhythm accented or softened as thought fitting; ornamentation decided upon; in legato (smoothly flowing) passages the amount and use of vibrato and portamento etc., be chosen; the tempo to be accelerated, retarded or kept steady; the voices in part music separated - all these and more are the flesh and blood of music.

A composer or editor can indicate his own interpretation of the music by adding conventional terms and symbols to the score, but these can only be a guide.   If a full interpretation were attempted the music would be so cluttered as to be virtually unreadable; a great deal has to be left to the performer.

Despite the importance of musical interpretation it is not really possible, nor indeed desirable, to teach this subject formally.   The best training is to listen to top class players.   Listen and learn, but do not necessarily copy slavishly.

Always remember that the simplest study played well is worth a great deal more than a difficult concert piece played badly.   There is a natural desire to progress to technically more demanding music but all too often this becomes obsessive.   The result is that so many amateur players rarely play anything really well.   The reader is there- fore recommended to spend at least an equal amount of time interpreting pieces he has mastered technically.   When struggling to get the right fingers to the right place at the right time it is virtually impossible to be "feeling" the music.

A piece of music must be made to live.   This is what music is all about.   On the other hand the performer's desire to express himself through his music must be tempered with study, particularly when playing music of byegone ages.   We all know how a twelve bar blues should sound and how it differs from a military march because they are contemporary musical forms which we hear daily on the radio, on television and in films.   But the differences between a Galliard and a Gavotte, or a Saraband and a Mazurca are not so commonly known.   If you wish to play music from the past it is both necessary and rewarding to read about its history and the characteristics of its basic rhythms and tempos.   Most public libraries have a good selection of music reference books.

SELECTED PIECES

In the following pages are a selection of pieces taken from the lists of the Associated Board of the Royal Schools of Music Grade III.   A candidate for this examination has to play one piece of his own choice from each of three lists.   He is also given a sight- reading test with music that is unfamiliar to him.   The full syllabus of all grades (I - VII) is obtainable free of charge from music shops and educational establishments. It should be pointed out that, though at the date of writing the pieces printed here have been in the lists for several years, the Board could make changes at any time.   In any case a student intending to sit this examination would need some coaching from a teacher and he would be familiar with the contemporary situation.

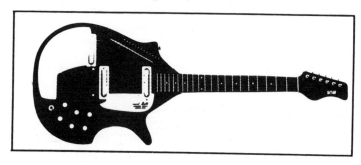

The Coral 'electric sitar' guitar

ADAGIO

Anonymous Baroque researched by Karl Scheit

MARCH

Diabelli

19th century right hand finger symbols:

+ = thumb
. = index
.. = middle
... = ring

STUDY

Matteo Carcassi

Study No. 3 from 25 Melodious and Progressive Studies opus 60

This is a beautiful piece of music in its own right but its purpose as a study is to develop the use of apoyando with arpeggio. The first note of the second and third triplets in each bar should be played apoyando. (Apoyando is when the striking finger, in this case the ring or third finger, comes to rest on the string below that being played. If the 1st string is being played the finger comes to rest on the 2nd string). The melody is thus made to sing out above the bass and middle accompaniment notes.

Lágrima

F. TARREGA

Packington's Pound

ANON

This dance tune dates from Shakespeare's time - the Renaissance.   It was the
practice in those days that when a section of music was marked to be repeated
the repeat was in the form of a variation.   Sometimes this was left to the
performer or, as in this example, the variations were written by the composer
or arranger.   The line marked A1 is a variation on that marked A.   The line
C1 is a variation on that marked C.

SCALES AND ARPEGGIOS FOR ASSOCIATED BOARD GRADE III

The study and practice of scales is most beneficial to players of any instrument. However, space does not permit this subject to be dealt with fully in this tutor because each major and minor scale and all the Modes can be played in one, two or three octaves and with a wide variety of fingerings.   Indeed the number and diversity of scales is even blanched at by the academic authorities who usually restrict scale studies to those most used in the Classical period, namely the major and minor.

The student who wishes to further his practical knowledge of the major and minor scales is recommended to one of the many books on the market which are devoted wholly to this subject.   Both the Associated Board of the Royal Schools of Music and the Trinity College of Music publish their own books of scales.

As an example of such studies here are the set scales and arpeggios for the Grade III examination of the Associated Board.   The fingering shown is that recommended by the Board, but any practical alternative is acceptable.

SCALES

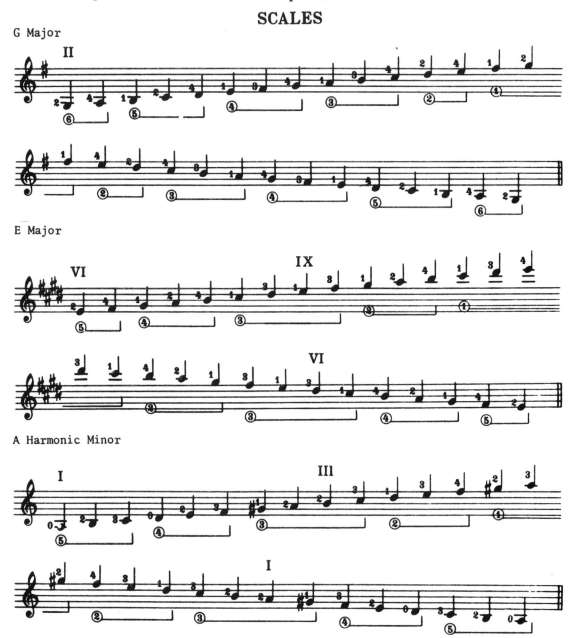

F# Harmonic Minor

ARPEGGIOS

C Major

A Major

B Minor

E Minor

THREE PIECES ONE FROM EACH OF THE LISTS FOR GRADE IV ASSOCIATED BOARD (1974)

Pavana muy llana para tañer

Diego Pisador
1552

slow

ADELITA

TARREGA

freely

STUDY

Study No. 7 from 25 Melodious & Progressive Studies opus 60

Matteo Carcassi

AN INTRODUCTION TO MODERN RHYTHM AND HARMONY

Contemporary popular and light music is largely based on harmonic developments
that took place during the Romantic period, 1820 - 1920.   The lush chords
that we find pleasing today would have sounded dissonant to musicians of the
Classical period (1750 - 1820).   Today we are also more adventurous in our use
of rhythm, influenced as we have been by the music of Africa and Latin America.
In the following pages you will find a brief discussion of some aspects of
modern rhythm and harmony, though no mention is made of "avant garde" atonal
music; this is so new it is difficult yet to tell the good from the bad.

TWO EXOTIC RHYTHMS - THE RHUMBA AND THE HABANERA

More and more today the guitarist is faced with exotic and unusual rhythms and time
signatures.   Many of these are only of importance to the specialist - for example, the
7/8 and 9/8 time signatures of Balkan and Greek folk tunes, the twelve beat compas of
much flamenco music, and the alternating 3/4, 6/8 rhythms of several South American
dances.   However, two such exotic rhythms, namely the Rhumba and the Habanera, have
become established in Western music and their widespread use makes some mention of them
most desirable.

The Habanera

The Habanera takes its name from Havana, Cuba, from where it is believed to have
originated.   Two famous Habaneras are Carmen's entrance song in Bizet's opera, and
La Paloma by Sebastian Yraider.   The Habanera is conventionally written in slow 2/4
time but is perhaps best thought of as having four beats in the bar, each beat being a
quaver.

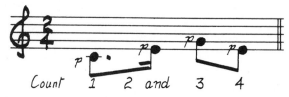

The rhythm of the Habanera is characterised by the dotted quaver/semi-quaver figure as
shown above.   It might help you to establish the rhythm if accompaniment notes are added
to the bass pattern thus:

Hold chord of C

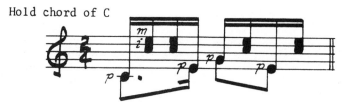

Melodies above this rhythmic bass often follow this pattern:

La Paloma (first phrase)

you should not have much difficulty playing this example because you probably know the
tune, but study it carefully so that you will recognise this somewhat awkward rhythm in
music with which you are not familiar.

A time signature of 4/4 means that there are four quarter notes (crotchets), or their equivalent in the bar.   In most Western European music this usually means that there are four beats in the bar.   However, the Latin American Rhumba has a 4/4 time signature but only three beats to the bar.   One bar is thought of as consisting of eight eighth notes (quavers) with the accents - or beats - falling on the 1st, 4th, and 7th thus:

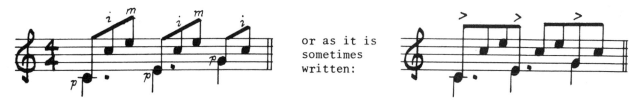

This is often counted

Here is a typical guitar arpeggio based on this rhythm.

or as it is sometimes written:

As can be seen the Rhumba consists of three beats: the first beat is a dotted crotchet, the second beat is a dotted crotchet, and the third beat a crotchet alone.   Here then is an idea alien to the West - a rhythm based on unequal beats - and as such it needs special care in notation and interpretation.

Melodies based on the Rhumba often follow this pattern.

Rhumba Cubana (first phrase)

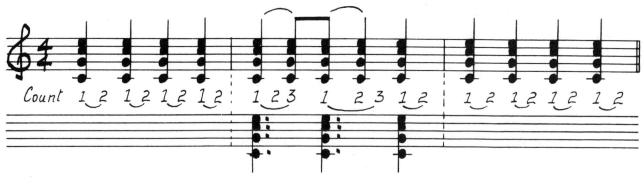

It should be noted that the Rhumba rhythm is sometimes written using tied notes, especially when it is used to syncopate one or two bars of music which has for the most part four beats to the bar - jazz and rock guitarists often use the Rhumba rhythm in this way.   For example:

The Bossa Nova

The basic rhythm of the Bossa Nova is one bar of the Rhumba followed by one bar of its mirror image, thus:

POPULAR RIFFS   (MORE ADVANCED RHYTHMIC STUDIES)

The foundation of much contemporary popular music is the Riff, a short rhythmic-melodic phrase that is repeated over and over again in much the same way as the Ground Bass of Classical music.   Because a Riff has to maintain interest despite constant repetition it is often rhythmically complex, and this is reflected in the number of rest signs, tied notes and triplets required in the notation of such music.   The selection of Riffs set out below therefore provide excellent studies in syncopated rhythm, a field largely ignored by Classical guitar composers.   Study each example carefully and if you experience real difficulty, and you might well do, then seek the assistance of either a teacher or musical friend.

Example No. 1 key A major

Example No. 2 key D major

Example No. 3 key E major (accompaniment to "La Bamba", "Guantanamera", "Twist and Shout")

Example No. 4 key E minor

Example No. 5 key A minor   Example No. 6 key A major

Example No. 7 key G major

Example No. 8 key A major

Example No. 9 key E major

Example No. 10 key E major

Example No. 11 key E minor (song theme - Michael Raven)

Example No. 12 key E major (Samba)

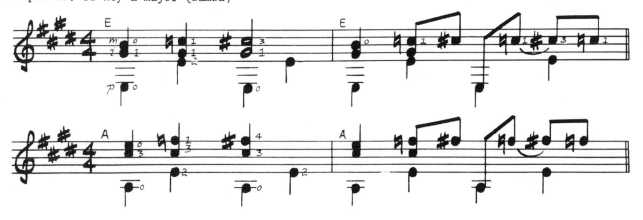

Example No. 13 key E major

STUDY IN SYNCOPATED RHYTHM

EYE LEVEL
(Theme from TV Series "Van der Valk")

Dutch traditional
arranged M. Raven

SOME IRREGULAR NOTE GROUPINGS

On Page 86 the triplet was fully discussed.   The triplet is not the only unusual grouping of notes; there are several others that the student should be familiar with, even though they are much less frequently used.   It should be noted that, like the triplet, most of these groupings involve the "squeezing in" of an extra note; but occasionally as in the example of the duplet given below, two or more notes have to be "stretched" to fill a time value longer than their value alone would indicate. Usually irregular groupings are written so that the complete unit is to be played in the time of one beat or, occasionally, two beats or a half beat; this means that though such groupings may look daunting in practice they rarely present any real problem.

When many notes have to be played on one beat ligado is often used.   In several of the examples below only the first note of each group need be plucked, the remaining notes being made to sound by hammering-on and pulling-off.

Duplet: a group of two notes occupying the time of three notes of the same value

Triplet: a group of three notes played in the time of two notes of the same value.

Quadruplet: a group of four notes occupying the time of three notes of the same value

Quintuplet: a group of five notes to be fitted into one beat or other time unit in which its number is irregular (e.g., five notes played in the time of 3 or 4 or 6).

Sextuplet: a group of six notes to be fitted into one beat or other time unit in which its number is irregular

Septuplet: a group of seven notes to be fitted into a beat or other time unit in which its number is irregular

138

MODERN CHORD SYMBOLS EXPLAINED

There are two methods of naming chords, the Classical and the Modern. In the Classical system a chord is named after the position of its root note in the scale. The triad based on the first note, or Tonic, is called I; that on the fifth note, or Dominant, is called V and so on.

In the Modern system a chord takes the letter name of its root note. Thus a major triad based on the note C is represented by a capital letter C. Any addition to or alteration of the major triad is indicated by qualifying symbols which define the intervals between all notes in relation to the root, or name note. Once the conventions are understood the symbol provides a complete description of the chord, no reference to any particular scale being necessary. In practice, however, many musicians tend to relate the symbols to the major scale of the name note of the chord (regardless of whether the chord is major or minor). In the following explanation each symbol is defined first by interval and second by reference to the major scale of the name note.

C means	the root plus the notes a major third and a perfect fifth above the root.
	The 1st, 3rd and 5th notes of the scale of C major (C E G).
Cm means	the root plus the notes a minor third and a perfect fifth above the root.
	The 1st, flattened 3rd, and 5th notes of the scale of C major (C E♭ G).
C6 means	the chord of C major plus the note a major sixth above the root.
	The 1st, 3rd, 5th and 6th notes of the scale of C major (C E G A).
Cm6 means	the chord of C minor plus the note a major sixth above the root.
	The 1st, flattened 3rd, 5th and 6th notes of the scale of C major (C E♭ G A).

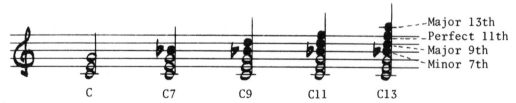

C   C7   C9   C11   C13

- - - Major 13th
--- Perfect 11th
- - - Major 9th
- - Minor 7th

Construction of chords based on the major triad with added minor 7th.

C7 means	the chord of C major plus the note a minor seventh above the root.
	The 1st, 3rd, 5th and flattened 7th notes of the scale of C major (C E G B♭).
C9 means	the chord of C major plus the notes a minor seventh and a major second (7 + 2 = 9) from the root.
	The 1st, 3rd, 5th, flattened 7th and 2nd notes of the scale of C major (C E G B♭ D). (Note sometimes the 7th is omitted)

C11 means | the chord of C major plus the notes a minor seventh and a perfect fourth (7 + 4 = 11) from the root. (The ninth shown in the musical explanation above is often omitted).

The 1st, 3rd, 5th and flattened 7th and 4th notes of the scale of C major (C E G B♭ F).

C13 means | the chord of C major plus the notes a minor seventh and a major sixth above the root (7 + 6 = 13). The ninth (2nd) and eleventh (4th) are often omitted.

The 1st, 3rd, 5th, flattened 7th and 6th notes of the scale of C major (C E G B♭ A).

Cm 7
Cm 9
Cm11
Cm13

These minor chords have the same construction as their major equivalents except that the interval of a third in the basic triad is minor. (For example Cm9 = C E♭ G B D).

C aug or C+ means | the chord of C major but with the fifth augmented, i.e., increased by a semitone.

The 1st, 3rd sharpened 5th notes of the scale of C major (C E G#).

C7 aug 5th means
or
C7 + 5

the chord of C major but with the fifth augmented and the addition of the note a minor seventh from the root.
The 1st, 3rd, sharpened 5th and flattened 7th notes of the scale of C major (C E G# B♭).

C7 dim 5th means
or
C7 ♭5

the chord of C major but with the fifth diminished (flattened) plus the note a minor seventh from the root.
The 1st, 3rd, flattened 5th and flattened 7th notes of the scale of C major (C E G♭ B♭).

C dim or C° means | the root plus the notes a minor third, a diminished fifth and a major sixth above, which together make a "circle" of notes all of which are separated by the interval of a minor third.

The 1st, flattened 3rd, flattened 5th and 6th notes of the scale of C major (C E♭ G♭ A).

C maj 7 means | the chord of C major plus the note a major seventh above the root.

The 1st, 3rd, 5th and 7th notes of the scale of C major (C E G B)

C sus 4 means | the chord of C major plus the note a perfect fourth above the root.

The 1st, 3rd, 5th and 4th notes of the scale of C major (C E G F).

The chord previous to C sus 4 is usually F major and the chord that follows is C major. The note F is suspended or left hanging over from the previous chord before resolution.

It should be noted that in the practical application of some of the more complex chords one or more of the notes are often omitted.

The reader may occasionally come upon symbols not mentioned in the table but in most cases these will give little problem.

THE PRACTICAL APPLICATION OF MODERN CHORDS

There is not space in this book to fully describe the practical application of these "modern" chords, but it is hoped that the following notes will be of some service.

1. Substitution

The seventh chords based on both major and minor triads are often used as substitute chords for the basic triad.   The choice of seventh depends largely on the style of music.   For example, in the Blues it is common to substitute C7 for C, F7 for F, etc. In Bossa Nova music and other sophisticated music it is common to substitute C major 7 for C, F major 7 for F etc.   In modern popular music the minor seventh is often substituted for the basic minor triad Dm becoming Dm7.

2. Passing Chords in Progressions.

Many "modern" chords occur as a result of a short melodic line which leads the ear from one fundamental chord to the next.

3.   Passing Chords in Repeating Motifs (Riffs)

The simple chord sequences found in much popular music are often made more interesting by decorating the individual chords with a repeating melodic phrase known in rock music as a riff.

Several more examples of such riffs are given elsewhere.

4.   Modulation

The chromatic nature of many of the chords under discussion makes them ideal for use as modulating chords when making a change from one key to another.   A succession of diminished chords for example can lead the composer from one key to any other however remote.

5.   Tone Colouring and Mood

Altered chords are used to create moods and heighten effects.   This is a vast field and the possibilities can only be hinted at.   Play the following example.   It is the accompaniment to the first few bars of a song by the author in which he wished to create a feeling of "a sunset by a peaceful sea-shore". *The sign ⁒ means repeat previous bar.*

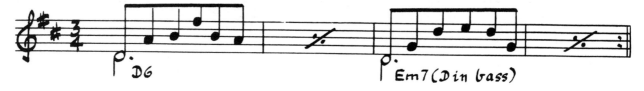

FOUR STUDIES IN MODERN HARMONY

No. 1 SOMEWHERE OVER THE RAINBOW

used with the kind permission of the copyright holder

Harburg/Arlen
arr. Almeida/Raven

142

No. 2   THE SONG FROM MOULIN ROUGE

used with the kind permission of the copyright holder

arranged Michael Raven

No. 3   HYMN A L'AMOUR

used with the kind permission of the copyright holder

arranged Michael Raven

144

No. 4   PETITE FLEUR

used with the kind permission of the copyright holder   arranged Michael Raven

This piece was written by the French jazz clarinetist, Sydney Bechet, (pronounced Behshay).   When played as a clarinet solo it is usually accompanied by a banjo playing chords - a steady four beats to the bar.   It is a beautiful tune, and gains a lot of its effect from the crotchet triplets of the melody which "fight against" the steady rhythm of the banjo.   To maintain the character of the piece the harmonic movement of the banjo chords have been kept, and indeed at many places elaborated upon.   The result is a very sophisticated piece of music.   There is a lot going on, and though not at all technically difficult the player must be very alert.   No chord symbols have been written because many of the chords are "altered" in jazz style.

For an explanation of crotchet triplets see page 86.

MOVEABLE CHORD SHAPES

Introduction

One of the great advantages of learning the theory of music is that a player can work out any chord, however unusual, in any position on the guitar.   Most players, and that includes many classical guitarists, do not however learn the theory of chords sufficiently well to be able to do this.   And yet you will see, and hear, many such players chording with an impressive ease.

They can do this because they have learnt the old jazz and dance band guitarists' trick of playing by moveable shapes and fret names.   Even when one can theoretically work out a chord it is often quicker in practice to use this well tried method.   All it involves is the learning of a few basic chord shapes, and the names of the notes on the first three strings of the guitar.   You do not have to be able to read music, just know the names of the notes.

Explanation

Any chord shape that requires three or more strings to be held down by the fingers of the left hand, is a moveable chord shape.   This means that by moving it up or down the fingerboard many different chords can be made using this one shape.   There are shapes for all types of chords - major, minor, 7th chords, and all the more sophisticated "modern" chords.

Here is a major chord shape

Wherever this shape is held on the fret board makes a major chord.   But as yet we have not given it a name.   In fact this shape is called a FIRST STRING MAJOR SHAPE.   The "first string" part of its name tells us that it will be called after the note held down on the first string.

name note

1st string

In this case the note is F (1st string, 1st fret).   So if you make this shape with the first string held down behind the first fret, the actual chord is F major.   Now, move that shape up two frets like this:

name note

You are now making the same shape but at the third fret.   So the chord will have a different name - the name of the note held down on the 1st string at the 3rd fret. This note is G.   The chord is therefore called G major.   So now we have made two major chords with one moveable shape.   Move it again to any of the other frets and you have more major chords.   But to give them a name you must learn the names of the notes on the first string.

Exactly the same reasoning applies to all the other moveable chord shapes.   Just to make certain that we understand, here is another shape:

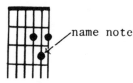

name note

It is a SECOND STRING MAJOR SHAPE.

Wherever you make this chord it will give you a major chord.   The exact name of the chord is given by the note held down on the second string.   This note is actually D (2nd string, 3rd fret), therefore the chord is called D major.

Incidentally, move this chord up so that the second string is being held down behind the sixth fret thus:

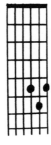

then the note on the second string is F, so we have made another chord of F major.   We have made the same actual chord but used a different shape.   We can make another chord of F using a 3rd string major shape.   Here are all three for comparison:

1st string shape	2nd string shape	3rd string shape
	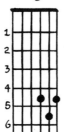	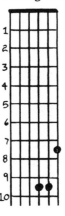

To complete this explanation, just one more example.   Slide down the 3rd string major shape so that the 3rd string is being stopped behind the 4th fret,

The note being made on the 3rd string is now B.   The chord is therefore called B major.

Just a word before you go on to learning a few shapes.   Most of these moveable chord shapes can be played in two or three different versions.   This should not confuse you. The first chart shows the easiest three string version of the shape.   The charts next to it in the same box show the same shape, but in its 4, 5 or 6 string form.   These are usually a little more difficult to play.   Learn the three string version first and then go back later and look at the fuller forms of the shape.   Only the most practical forms of the shapes are given.   Note also that it is necessary to change the fingering sometimes when changing from the three string version to the extended forms.

Symbols Used

Numerals indicate suggested fingering of the left hand.   1 = index, 2 middle, 3 ring, 4 little.   This sign ⌐‾‾‾¬ means barre; the index finger lies across all the strings thus bracketed.

148

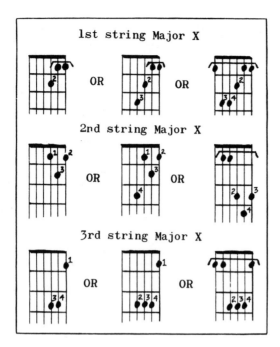

1st string Major X — 2nd string Major X — 3rd string Major X

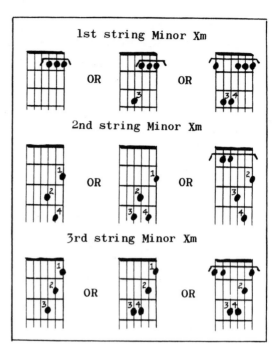

1st string Minor Xm — 2nd string Minor Xm — 3rd string Minor Xm

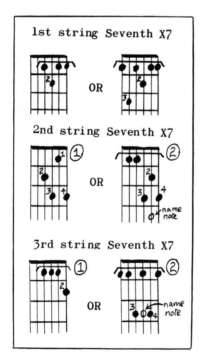

1st string Seventh X7 — 2nd string Seventh X7 — 3rd string Seventh X7

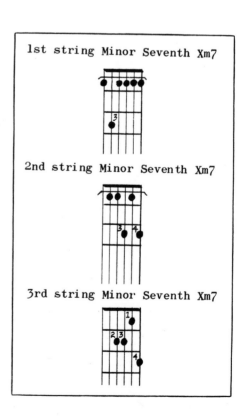

1st string Minor Seventh Xm7 — 2nd string Minor Seventh Xm7 — 3rd string Minor Seventh Xm7

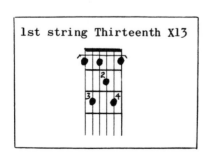

1st string Thirteenth X13

149

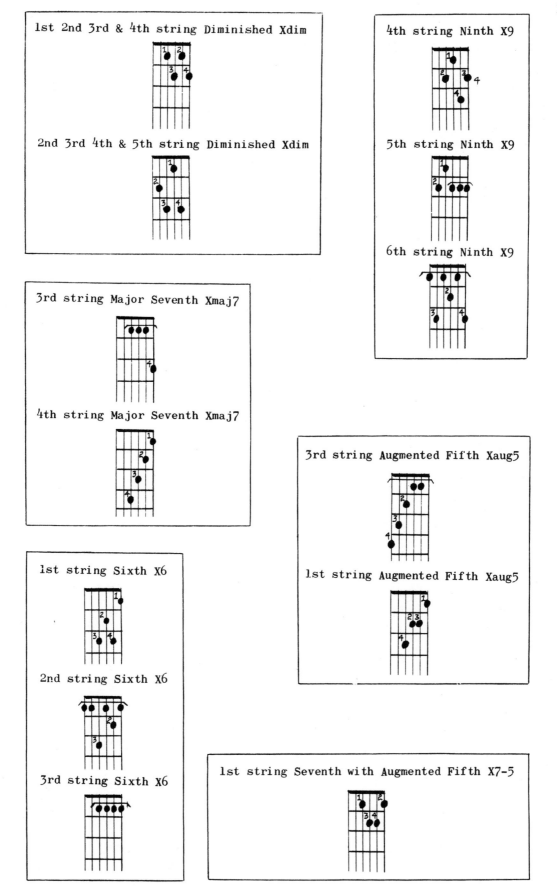

THE CAPO D'ASTRO OR CEJILLA

The capo is a device that is used to raise the pitch of the strings of the guitar. It avoids the necessity of retuning if it is desired to raise the pitch of a whole piece of music. It is therefore a transposing instrument.

There are a variety of capos available today. Undoubtedly the most suitable for nylon strung guitars are those made of elastic. The drawing shows a capo of this kind in position on a guitar. Elastic capos are light, do not damage the guitar neck, and can be shifted from position to position without having to be removed.

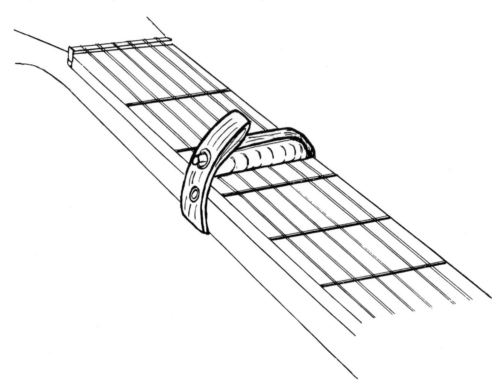

Flamenco, folk and blues guitarists use capos very frequently. A capo is virtually indispensable in accompaniment work of any complexity. Imagine for example that you have learned an accompaniment to a song and that it is of a technical difficulty equal to a concert guitar solo, as is often the case in flamenco. Suppose now that a singer says, "I'm sorry but the key of E major is too low for me, I always sing this song in the key of F sharp major." A good pianist would be able to transpose at sight, but for technical reasons this is impossible on the guitar - even for Segovia. The impossible is made possible by the use of a capo. By placing this device behind the second fret the guitarist can then play note for note the arrangement he has already learned. The capo will transpose the music one tone higher, from E major to F sharp major. What is more, if on another occasion a different singer wished to sing the same song in the key of G major, all the guitarist has to do is place the capo at the third fret. The music will then be transposed up by a tone and a half (three semitones).

The capo is often used for another reason. The guitar is a low pitched instrument and this gives it a mellow unobtrusive sound. Normally this is ideal for an accompanying role but sometimes a brighter more forceful sound is required. One way of achieving this is by raising the pitch, and this can be done by using a capo. Flamenco and folk guitarists often use the capo for exactly this reason, even when playing guitar solos. A flamenco guitarist in particular has often to play with a background noise of people eating, drinking and talking. The increase in pitch and therefore brightness obtained by using a capo allows him to cut through such background sounds.

However, the most important use of the capo is as a transposing instrument. Even simple song accompaniments can be very difficult to perform effectively in some "awkward" keys. You will not find a single classical guitar solo in such keys as D flat minor, or E flat major, so it is unreasonable to expect a guitarist to provide an effective accompaniment. in such "unguitarlike" keys. But in practice the problem is resolved by the use of a capo.

Below is a chart showing the effect of using a capo at different frets. Remember that every note and every chord is raised by a semitone every time the capo is moved up one fret. The third string is tuned to the note G. Place a capo behind the first fret the actual pitch of the new "open" string is G sharp (or its enharmonic A flat). Likewise the chord of G major becomes G sharp major (or its enharmonic A flat major).

Chart showing the effect of using a Capo on the Common Chords of the keys of C major and A minor

open	C	F	G7	Am	Dm	E7
Capo at 1st fret	C# or Db	F# or Gb	G#7 or Ab7	A#m or Bbm	D#m or Ebm	F7
2nd fret	D	G	A7	Bm	Em	F#7 or Gb7
3rd fret	D# or Eb	G# or Ab	A#7 or Bb7	Cm	Fm	Gm
4th fret	E	F	B7	C#m or D m	F#m or Gbm	G#m or Abm
5th fret	F	F# or G	C7	Dm	Gm	Am

(a capo is not normally used above the 5th fret)

Looking at this chart we see that if we place a capo behind the third fret and play 'C shapes' (C F and G7), we are actually playing in the key of Eb. What is otherwise a very difficult key on the guitar therefore becomes easy. The chord of C has been transposed up to Eb, the chord of F to Ab and the chord of G7 to Bb 7.

You could make similar charts for each key. But it is better to understand the principle and work out the effect of using a capo in each individual case.

Using a capo it is possible to make the common chords of every key with only the nut position shapes of the common chords of the keys of C major and A minor, and G major and E minor.

Chart Showing the effect of using a capo on the Common Chords of the keys of G major and E minor

open	G	C	D7	Em	Am	B7
Capo at 1st fret	G# or Ab	C# or Db	D#7 or Eb7	Fm	A#m or Bbm	C7
2nd fret	A	D	E7	F#m or Gbm	Bm	C#7 or Db7
3rd fret	A# or Bb	D# or Eb	F7	Gm	Cm	D7
4th fret	B	E	F#7 or Gb7	G#m or Abm	C#m or Dbm	D#7 or Eb7
5th fret	C	F	G7	Am	Dm	E7

Use of the Capo with two guitars

It is very common these days for two or more guitars to be played together to provide a chordal rhythmic background to either vocal or instrumental music. In such situations a capo can be used on one guitar to enable the same chords to be played at different positions, thus filling out the sound.

For example, if the music is in the key of E major, one guitar can play in 'E shapes' without a capo and another can play in 'C shapes' with a capo placed behind the fourth fret.

AN INTRODUCTION TO FOLK-BLUES GUITAR

In recent years a distinctive style of guitar playing has been developed. It is known
variously as pattern-picking, clawhammer or folk fingerstyle, and is the basis of much
folk, blues and ragtime guitar music.   Though this book is primarily concerned with
Classical technique the contemporary popularity and usefulness of this style makes
some mention of it most desirable.

One of the basic techniques of "folk guitar" is that known in Classical circles as the
Alberti Bass.   A tune is harmonised with the minimum basic chords and the bass notes
of these chords are picked out to provide a regular pulsing beat.   This bass is most
important.   It serves three functions, (a) it provides a bass, (b) it provides the
harmony (because the bass notes are derived from the chords), and (c) it provides the
beat, or rhythm.

The fingers are thus left free either to play a regular repeating pattern as an
accompaniment to a song, or to play the tune - which is in fact often forced into the
pattern used for accompaniment, thus technically playing not the tune but a variation
upon it.

A distinctive feature of "folk guitar" is the syncopation caused by forcing the melody
(finger) notes on to the off beat.   This comes quite naturally with this style but if
it were written theoretically correctly it would often confuse the reader because a
plethora of tied notes would have to be used.   For this reason notation of this music
is simplified.   This is made possible because the music is based on chord shapes which
are usually held for one or more complete bars and it is accepted that all notes played
are sustained for the duration of the shape or until cut off by the playing of another
on the same string.   This will be made clear by means of an example:

Example 1.

Conventionally written   hold a chord of C

"correctly" written

As you can see it would be almost perverse to write this music in the "correct" way.
Even skilled sight readers would find the going difficult.

The pattern shown in Example 1 is very commonly used for accompaniment work, it being
repeated over and over, changing chord as necessary.   Here is another very widely
used pattern.

Example 2.   153

This pattern is especially useful for melody playing.   Again, the left hand holds the
necessary chords, the passing notes of the melody not contained in the chords being
fingered as required - usually by the little finger which in this style of playing
tends to be very busy.   It should be understood that a melody is often altered
rhythmically to fit the pattern.   The result is in effect a syncopated instrumental
variation. (see p. 158)

The great advantage of this clawhammer style is that very little knowledge of musical
theory is required for very acceptable results to be obtained.   A good ear, a handful
of chords; personal contact with others of greater proficiency from whom tricks of the
trade can be prised; the will to spend many hours in trial and error experiment; and
the concept of the Alberti bass constitute the road taken by many skilled professional
performers in the folk-blues style.   Players with this kind of background naturally
develop highly individual styles.   There is no one correct or established way to play
a particular tune, rather are there as many ways as there are performers.   This can
be confusing to the classically orientated player who is used to working from the
definitive written score, though in Renaissance times there was a similar freedom of
approach.   An increasing amount of folk-blues material has been notated and published
in recent years.   Have no hesitation when working on such music to make what
alterations or additions you might think fitting - for whatever reason.   You might
even simplify passages of the written music because it is technically beyond you -
this is quite acceptable, and is in keeping with the spirit and style of the music,
for above all else you must not let technical difficulties interfere with the flow and
movement of the piece.   Make an arrangement that gives you pleasure and satisfaction
to play whilst practising alternative technically demanding passages to be included at
a later date.

An aspect of folk-blues playing that is often not fully appreciated by classically
trained players is the rhythmical approach which is fundamental to this style.   The
accent in classical music is on melody and harmony; the accent in folk-blues is on
rhythm.   The notation of a solo by a ragtime or blues guitarist can sometimes look
very "empty" - not very much appears to be going on.   But hear the same thing played
and it can seem a different piece of music.   The "swing" "beat" or "pulse" so
inherent in this style is almost impossible to capture in written notation.

One point of technique important to the performance of the blues is the slurred or
"bent" note.   In this case slur does not mean hammering-on or pulling-off but the
violent distortion of the note by pushing the string either to or from the player.   The
pitch of the note can be "bent" up anything from a micro quarter tone to a whole tone.
This gives the characteristic wailing sound so common in modern pop music.

It should be mentioned that though the nylon strung guitar can be used in the
performance of folk-blues music, a more authentic sound is obtained from steel strings.
They are brighter, have a crisper attack, more sustain and are easier to "bend".   Today
most players use light gauge strings which are very easy to hold down and can be made to
slap the frets with little effort.   This string slapping, when used with discretion,
can add to the rhythmic feel and attack - it creating a staccato drum like sound to notes
played.

Ladies don't go a Thievin'

as recorded on the L.P. Death and the Lady, Folk Heritage FHR 047,

by Michael Raven and Joan Mills

Words: 19th century broadside
Tune: Dave Moran
Guitar accompaniment: M. Raven

fairly fast

little finger
left hand

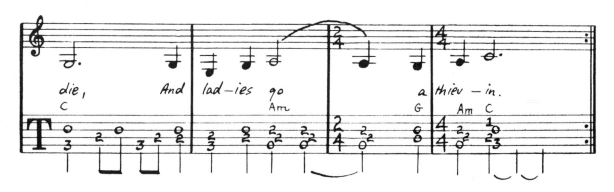

GEORGIA RAG

Trad. arr. M.Raven

156

The Triplet in "The Blues"

The lilt or swing characteristic of much blues music is derived from its trochaic ("in threes") rhythm.   This is conventionally written in four-four time using triplets but when a whole piece is played using triplets it could equally well have been written in six-eight time.   The only difference would be in the value attributed to the beat note.

If you keep a steady beat by tapping your foot you can either think of the beat as being worth a crotchet or a dotted crotchet.   If you then sing notes in threes above the beat thus: Count   1 2 3   1 2 3   1 2 3   1 2 3
        Beat   x   x   x   x   then this can be written in two ways,

The sound is exactly the same, only the method of writing is different.   Similarly:

Why then is such music written in 4/4 time triplets, which are less familiar to the musician than six-eight time?   Simply convention.   Music that uses triplets throughout can be thought of as six-eight.   It has the same feel and musical sound.

Twelve Bar Blues accompaniment pattern   Trad. arranged M. Raven

TWELVE BAR BLUES

M. Raven

POPULAR STUDY IN CLAWHAMMER 1975

Steets of London from the playing of Ralph MacTell.

AN INTRODUCTION TO FLAMENCO GUITAR

The world of flamenco is a world unto itself. It is possible to dabble with flamenco and learn some typical guitar solos but to achieve any real satisfaction from this music demands dedication above the ordinary. This is because flamenco is an amalgam of the singing, dancing, and instrumental work of a race alien to the West. Flamenco is the music of the Spanish gipsy, a people who migrated from Northern India and settled in Spain as recently as the 15th century. Flamenco retains a distinctly Oriental flavour, what is more the Spanish people themselves owe a great deal of their distinctive culture to the fact that the Moors occupied their land for 700 years until finally driven out by Ferdinand and Isabella at the end of the 15th century. Quite literally as one Eastern race was driven out to the south another, the gipsies, entered from the north. The national culture of Spain quite simply owes more to the East than the West. Because of this there is only one way for the non-Spaniard to learn flamenco satisfactorily and that is to go to Spain, learn the language and be taught by, and play with, genuine indigenous performers.

Having said this the author must immediately qualify his statement for there are today two kinds of flamenco. There is traditional flamenco, in which the guitar plays an accompanying role to the singing and dancing, and solo concert flamenco guitar which is a modern phenomenon that owes as much to Classical music as its gipsy roots. The modern solo flamenco guitarist still uses traditional rhythms and forms but increasingly there is a tendency to include music from other cultures, adapting it by using flamenco techniques. In actual fact this is in keeping with the spirit of flamenco which has always been adding to its traditional forms. The difference is that today the solo guitarist is playing arrangements of popular music from other countries that have not been adopted by flamenco singers and dancers. He has also adapted and expanded his techniques. The fast arpeggios and the tremolo for example have no place in traditional flamenco for the practical reason that they would be inaudible above the hand clapping, foot stamping, and singing of the other performers. The main function of the traditional guitarist is to provide a strong rhythmic backing for dancers and singers. Even in sad, quiet songs where the guitar has no problem of projection it should remain unobtrusive and provide an accompaniment - not make a duet with the singer. It might be said that a traditional flamenco guitarist is judged not so much by what he does, as what he does not do. He has to be tasteful and restrained.

Not so the modern concert performer. He is a one-man show who all too often feels he must "dazzle" an audience by his virtuosity. A slow Soleares will be concluded by a fast Bulerias. He will imitate a Paraguayan harp, or play a New Orleans boogie, or even arrangements of popular songs of the day. There is a place for such music and it is unfair to criticise such a performer on the grounds that he is "bastardising" his art. He is not so much betraying his tradition as adapting it to a new situation, and very often the best "new music" players are skilful accompanists in the traditional style. There are in fact two kinds of flamenco guitar, the old and the new.

The new style is obviously more suited to players of non-Spanish origin. They can borrow the techniques, the spirit and attack of the traditional style and use them for their own purposes. Following this introduction to flamenco guitar you will find a discussion of the most characteristic technique used in flamenco, namely Rasgueado; but no attempt can be made here to describe flamenco forms and rhythms in any depth for two reasons.

First to be of any value it would require a book of this size to be entirely devoted to the subject, and several of these already exist; and second that more than any other music, flamenco must be taught by a live teacher for certain techniques are virtually impossible to describe. The attack and rhythmic feeling so essential to the performance of flamenco have to be imbued by a living presence.

NOTE: Flamenco guitar as we know it today was made possible by the work of one man above all others - namely Ramon Montoya, who was the first to show the possibilities of the flamenco guitar as a solo instrument. He played in a lyrical style and avoided the excessive speed and showmanship that characterises some modern players. Probably the greatest living flamenco guitarist is Sabicas, a player of unmatched technique and great musical taste.

RASGUEADO TECHNIQUE

Rasgueado is the collective name for the several techniques used to rhythmically strum the strings of the guitar and the allied techniques of damping and tapping.

Rasgueado produces one of the most characteristic and individual sounds of the guitar and has been widely used in all kinds of music from Renaissance pavans and galliards to flamenco and contemporary popular music. (In passing it should be mentioned that the term used to cover the various plucking techniques is "punteado"). Since late Baroque times rasgueado has been almost totally ignored by composers of art music whereas "the people" have taken full advantage of its distinctive sound and rhythmic power. When a strong rhythmic/harmonic sound pattern is desired there is no better combination than chords played on the guitar in rasgueado style.

Before describing the various rasgueado techniques it should be stressed that this is a field in which live instruction by a teacher is essential if a proper understanding is to be achieved. This is not because rasgueado is particularly difficult but because the written symbols need to be related to the actual sound for the player to achieve the proper "attack" and rhythmic nuance. When playing rasgueado be bold. The strings must be struck sharply and cleanly - they must be attacked.

1.   The Downstroke with the Index Finger

The index finger strikes down, towards the floor, across the strings the player wishes to sound, usually at least four and often all six. The right forearm and hand do not move, only the index finger. The finger must strike strongly and cleanly - the back of the nail is punched down so that all the strings sound almost instantaneously. The down-stroke is notated in music by an arrow next to the chord thus:

The arrow indicates that the index finger strikes down from the bass strings to the treble. NOTE: To steady the right hand many flamenco guitarists rest the thumb on the sixth string, this also helps to stop beginners from moving the forearm and hand.

2.   The Upstroke with the Index Finger

The index finger strikes up, towards the player. Usually the upstroke is on an unaccented beat (though not always) and tends to produce a slightly weaker sound than the downstroke. Usually only the top three or four strings are made to sound. Again, only the finger moves, the hand and forearm remain stationary. Be careful not to dig the finger into the strings. It must glide over them quite freely, the tip of the finger bowing slightly outwards as it meets the resistance of the strings. The upstroke is notated in music by an arrow next to the chord thus:

The arrow indicates that the index finger strikes up from the treble strings towards the bass.

3.   The Roll (Spanish "redondo")

This is the most difficult technique to describe verbally and can only be satisfactorily learned from a live teacher by demonstration.

The right hand fingers are curled into the palm of the hand.   Commencing with the little finger each finger executes a downstroke.   One finger follows quickly after the other. The little finger brushes down and before it has completed its movement the ring finger follows it, succeeded by the middle finger and finally the index finger on which the accent is placed.   The result should be a sound similar to a drum roll.   The Roll falls naturally into two parts; in the roll lasting for a value of one crotchet the actions of the first three fingers, ℓ a m (ℓ = little finger) take approximately a quaver and the index finger striking down last rings out for a quaver thus:

The roll is a complex musical effect and is never written out in full.   Different authors use different symbols to represent it, but you should always find an explanation in the introduction of any particular book or piece of music.   Here are the two most commonly used methods of indicating the Roll.

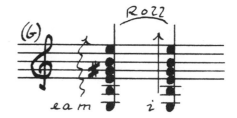

Method (b) may look unnecessarily complicated but in practice is much the better for accurate notation.   This is because the roll often starts on an "off-beat" and ends on the "on-beat".   For example:

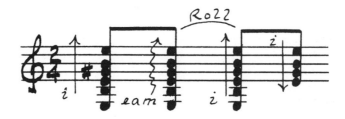

Method (b) also makes it easier to differentiate between the roll ending with a downstroke and the roll ending with an upstroke (discussed below).   When a roll lasts for two beats the same symbol is used; the time values are merely doubled thus:

4.   The Roll ending with an Upstroke

The fingers strike down rapidly one after the other, commencing with the little finger, just as described in 3 above; but the index finger, after completing its downstroke, returns very quickly with an upstroke.   This gives the roll an extra crispness and snap. The extra action does <u>not</u> extend the duration of the roll; it is "crammed in" at the end. The upstroke takes a <u>half</u> of the value of the roll as a whole, just as the index finger's downstroke did in the ordinary roll described in 3.

This roll can be notated thus:

5.   The Downstroke with the Thumb

The thumb can be run down across the strings from the bass to treble in two ways. (a) If brushed down quickly all the strings sound almost instantaneously.   (b) If brushed down slowly the effect is to arpeggio the notes of the chord.

6.   The Upstroke with the Thumb

When a loud, powerful upstroke is required the thumb can be used.   The strings are made to sound by being struck with the back of the thumb nail.

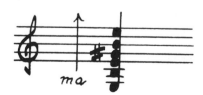

7.   The Downstroke using the Middle and Ring Fingers

When an extra loud powerful downstroke is required the middle and ring fingers can strike down together as a unit - not separately but with the finger tips touching and striking together.   This downstroke is usually used in conjunction with the thumb upstroke (6). Flamenco guitarists use this combination at the end of a piece to obtain maximum volume to create a final crescendo.

8.   The Roll ending with the Thumb Downstroke

The roll is performed just as described in 3 above but ends with an accented downstroke
of the thumb.   As in the roll ending with an index finger upstroke this additional
action does not extend the duration of the roll.

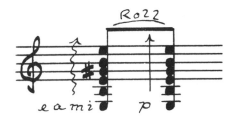

In notation this roll can be indicated thus:

9.   The Continuous Roll using only the Fingers

The most common method of performing the continuous roll is as follows: the fingers
execute an ordinary roll and as each finger completes its downstroke it immediately
commences an upstroke.   This means that as the last fingers ($m\,i$), are completing
their downstrokes, the first fingers ($\ell\,a$) are beginning their upstrokes.   This action
is repeated without a break for as long as is required.   The result is a continuous
sound.   This technique needs a great deal of practice before a smooth, regular,
continuous sound is achieved.   This effect is usually indicated in written music by the
words "continuous roll" or "continuous rasg." and a wavy arrow, thus:

10.   The Continuous Roll using the Thumb

The fingers perform an ordinary roll and on completion the thumb strikes up with the
back of the nail; these actions are repeated without interruption for as long as the note
value indicated.   This technique is used when a very fast strong continuous roll is
required.

11.   The Tap, or Golpé

The soundboard of the guitar can be tapped by the right hand fingers to produce a
variety of percussive effects.   Very often the fingers, usually the ring finger but
sometimes the little finger, tap the soundboard below the strings to fill in missing
beats or half beats.   Such taps are often used to syncopate the rhythm and in effect
take the place of periods of silence (indicated by rest signs and made by damping the
strings).   The tap is notated by either a cross X, or a box □ , or the circled letter
name of the tapping finger - e.g. ⓐ, or the letter G, meaning golpé (Spanish for tap).

Sometimes the thumb taps the soundboard above the strings.

164

12. The Tap, or Golpé used as an Accent

The ring finger (or little finger) can tap the soundboard in unison with a downstroke of the index finger. As the index finger strikes the strings so does the tapping finger strike the soundboard. This technique is often used by flamenco guitarists to stress the accented beats of a rhythm. (Remember that flamenco guitars have protective plastic sheets called golpeadores fixed to the soundboard). This effect is notated as in 11 above. The symbol is placed above the chord with which it is to be played. For example:

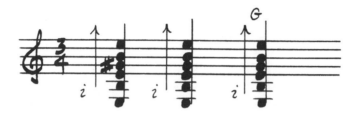

13. Alzapua

Alzapua is the Spanish name for a technique used in both Renaissance art music and contemporary flamenco whereby the treble strings are made to sound by being struck with alternating up and down strokes with the thumb. This technique can be applied to either one string alone, or two, or three strings together. It is indicated in written music thus:

14. Damping, with the Right Hand

Beats or half beats of silence can be made by damping the strings. The palm of the right hand falls flat across all the strings so stopping them from vibrating. Sometimes this damping action is converted into a mild percussive sound by making the strings slap against the fretboard and then silenced. There are no special symbols to indicate the damp or the slap; the silence is notated by a rest sign.

15. Parado

Parado is the Spanish name for a technique used by flamenco guitarists to damp the strings by using the little finger of the <u>left</u> hand. It is usually only employed with nut position chord shapes which do not require the use of the little finger. The procedure is as follows.

A chord shape is held and the strings made to sound. The sound is killed almost immediately by placing the left hand little finger, which is held straight from the knuckle joint, flat across all six strings. The little finger does not have to exert much pressure; it merely has to stop the strings vibrating. With a little practice the chord can be "cut" very sharply and cleanly. Sometimes the left hand fingers holding the chord shape also release their pressure on the strings, but this is not at all necessary.

This method of damping the strings is used for playing chords staccato. There is no special symbol; the conventional staccato sign of a dot placed above or below the chord being considered sufficient. Parado is treated as an ornament to be used at the discretion of the player.

As can be seen this is quite an armoury of techniques. Many hundreds of rhythms can be made by selecting and applying these methods of striking the strings, and a variety of rhythmic nuances obtained which are special to the guitar and defy impersonation by other instruments.

Here are a few examples of the use of the rasgueado techniques.   Each pattern is designed to be repeated over and over, changing chord as required.

1.   The Basic Strum

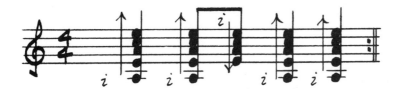

2.   Calypso

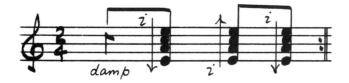

3.   Martial

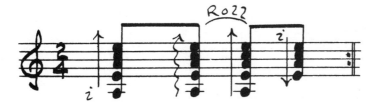

4.   Bolero

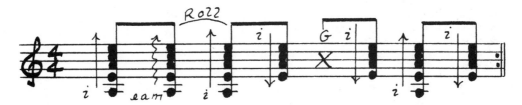

5.   Folk Strum

6.   Latin Waltz

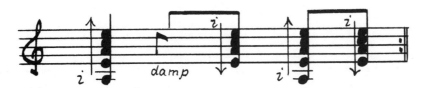

CARACOLES

FLAMENCO GUITAR SOLO

Spanish trad. arr. M. Raven

The basic rasgueado and four falsettas of the Caracoles (an Alegrias in C major)

The Caracoles has the same rhythm and basic rasgueado as the Soleares

THE GREAT STAVE AND THE BASS CLEF

The range of sounds produced by the human voice from bass to soprano and by most musical instruments can be written on a stave of eleven lines.   These form the Great Stave.

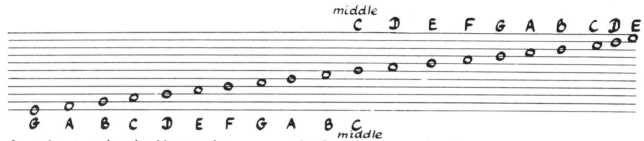

In order to make the lines and spaces on the Great Stave easier to read they are divided into two smaller staves of five lines each.   The missing line ------ middle C is written using a ledger line.

The two smaller staves are distinguished one from the other by Clef signs.

The Treble Clef

The upper five lines are marked by the treble or G clef.   (The lower curl of the sign commences on the line representing the note G).   This is the clef used for all guitar music.

The Bass Clef

The lower five lines are marked by a bass or F clef.   (The two dots are placed either side of the line representing the note F).   The bass clef is used in music that has many deep bass notes that would otherwise require excessive use of leger lines.

Piano music is written using both the bass clef and the treble clef.   A guitarist will find this rather strange, and unless he wishes to play bass guitar there is little need to learn the notes of the bass clef in the same way that he must learn those of the treble clef.   However, the notes of the bass clef can be named by application of a very simple rule.   That is: "To read music in the bass clef as though it were in the treble clef raise each note by one line, or space".

For example:

Bass Clef   Treble Clef

When transcribing bass clef notes to the treble in this way remember that you have raised them by two octaves.   Having established the names of the notes in this way they would be lowered either one or two octaves to place them on the bass strings of the guitar.

MICHAEL RAVEN CATALOGUE

If you experience any difficulty in obtaining these books from your local music shop they can be supplied to you post free direct from the publisher:

Michael Raven, Yew Tree Cottage, Jug Bank, Ashley, Market Drayton, Shropshire, TF9 4NJ
Tel: 01630 672304

Note: all cassettes cost £6.50.

GUITAR MUSIC

The Complete Guitarist
Michael Raven
Price £12.00
Universally acclaimed by the trade press as "the finest classical guitar tutor available today." Follows the Associated Board syllabus. Introductions to folk-blues and flamenco. Assumes no prior knowledge. Classical and modern harmony and special techniques explained in great detail. Includes 64 complete solos which range from lute music to classical studies and arrangements of popular songs. "Unreservedly recommended," Charles Scott, *Classical Guitar*. 9th edition, 172 pages, A4 size.

The Guitarist's Good Book
Michael Raven
Price £7.50
Easy arrangements of 82 well known songs, traditional tunes and hymns. Complete with words and chord symbols for those who wish to strum simple accompaniments. Widely used by absolute beginners. Staff notation only. The solo guitar arrangements provide useful alternative study material. "Detailed instructions, excellent arrangements, tremendous value for money... unreservedly recommended." *Fretwire* A4 size, 96 pages.

Popular Songs for Guitar 1
Michael Raven
Price £4.50
First published in 1976 and still going strong. Easy but musically satisfying arrangements of 15 timeless tunes: Danny Boy, Minuetto Allegretto, Now the Carnival is Over, Plaisir d'Amour, Morning has Broken, Return to Sorento, Those were the Days, Scarborough Fair, Amazing Grace, Guantanamera, Midnight in Moscow, etc. All the music is printed in both staff notation and tablature. 32 pages, A4 size. **Companion Cassette:** all the music in book 1 is on Side One of the cassette. On Side Two is all the music in Popular Songs for Guitar book 2. Total playing time 46 minutes.

Popular Songs for Guitar 2
Michael Raven
Price £4.50
Another 17 well known tunes amongst which are two of the Rodrigo Guitar Concerto themes and a performance arrangement of The Entertainer. Other tunes include El Condor Pasa, The Sloop John B, Waltzing Matilda and Viva Espana. All the music is in both staff notation and tablature. 32 pages. A4 size. **Companion Cassette:** all the music of book 2 is on Side Two of the cassette. On Side One is all the music in Book 1. Total playing time 46 minutes.

Popular Tunes for Guitar 1
Michael Raven
Price £4.50
Easy but musically satisfying solo guitar arrangements of eight popular tunes - The Green Leaves of Summer (from the film The Alamo), With God on our Side (Bob Dylan), Portsmouth (Mike Oldfield), Wooden Heart (Elvis Presley), etc. All the music is in both staff notation and tablature. Also included is the popular concert solo by Michael Raven, A Welsh Fantasy. 32 pages, A4 size. **Companion Cassette:** all the music in this book is on Side One of the cassette together with recordings of Eight Traditional Tunes in Tabla-ture. On Side Two is the music to Book 2. Playing time 60 minutes.

Popular Tunes for Guitar 2
Michael Raven
Price £4.50
A selection of 16 well known tunes in easy solo guitar arrangements. Titles include: Never on a Sunday, theme from the Onedin Line, Masters of War, Lord of the Dance, It's a Long Way to Tipperary, House of the Rising Sun, Limelight etc. Printed here too is Choro y Danza, a full scale concert guitar solo by Michael Raven. All the music is in both staff notation and tablature. 32 pages, A4 size. **Companion Cassette:** all the music in this book is recorded on Side Two of the cassette. On Side One is the music to Book 1.

Eight Traditional Tunes in Tablature
Michael Raven
Price £1.50
These arrangements of 8 attractive little tunes make few technical demands. 8 pages, A4 size. **Companion Cassette:** these tunes are recorded at the end of Side One on the Popular Tunes for Guitar Books 1 and 2 cassette.

A Variety of Guitar Music 1
Michael Raven
Price £7.50
67 pieces: 16th and 17th Century dances; Classical and Romantic music; folk tunes; flamenco solos and ragtime and blues. This book has been in print since 1968 and was the first collection

that we published. All the music is in tablature, and most is also in staff notation. "It has a rhyme and reason all its own." *Stephan Grossman*. 80 pages A4 size. **Recording:** some of the music is played by Michael Raven on the CD, *Retrospective*.

A Variety of Guitar Music 1 (Revised)
Michael Raven
Price £7.50
A selection of pieces from the original best-selling book, redrawn and printed in both staff notation and tablature, except for the long flamenco Soleares which is in tablature only. 64 pages, A4 size. **Recording:** Much of the music has been recorded on the *Retrospective* CD and on other albums.

A Variety of Guitar Music 2
Michael Raven
Price £5.00
Music in a variety of styles: Buckdancer's Choice, El Paso Waltz, Ragtime Annie, Wilson's Wild, Coventry Carol, March of Brian Boru, Alegrias (a full length flamenco guitar solo) etc. Most pieces are only of moderate difficulty. All the music is printed in staff notation and tablature. 40 pages, A4 size. **Companion Cassette:** all the music note for note as printed is recorded on Side One of the cassette. On Side Two is all the music printed in The Chant of Falsity (see below). Playing time 70 minutes.

A Variety of Guitar Music 3
Michael Raven
Price £7.50
30 solos in a variety of styles including a set of original compositions by Michael Raven and an "off the record" transcription of the magnificent Tarantos, a show stopping flamenco guitar solo of 5 minutes' duration, first recorded by Michael Raven on the LP A Miscellany of Guitar Music. All the music is in both tablature and staff notation. 64 pages A4 size. **Companion Cassette:** all the music, note for note as printed. Duration approximately 50 minutes.

The Chant of Falsity
Michael Raven
Price £4.50
25 pieces in many different styles. This is really another Variety of Guitar Music. The titles include Rhumba Habanera, Moorish Zambra, a set of four colourful Sevillanas dances from Spain, Rag in C major, Sage Leaf, Give me your Hand (a lovely Irish aire), Mozart Quadrille, Villanella etc. All the music is printed in both staff notation and tablature. 32 pages, A4 size. **Companion Cassette:** all the music in this book is recorded on Side Two of the cassette; on Side One is recorded the contents of A Variety of Guitar Music Book 2. Total playing time 70 minutes.

English Folk Guitar 1
Michael Raven
Price £7.50
Devoted almost entirely to song accompaniment with off-the-record transcriptions of pieces by Nic Jones and arrangements in the style of Martin Carthy and many others. Words to all the songs; melody lines in staff notation; guitar part in tablature; details of 10 different tunings; tablature thoroughly explained; 29 songs each with an analytical commentary. The first and still the only book devoted to the subject. 72 page, A4 size. **Recordings:** there is not a companion cassette but Death and the Lady, The Jolly Highwayman, The Captain's Apprentice and Ladies Don't go a Thieving are available on The Folk Heritage Recordings, a compilation of two LPs recorded by Michael Raven and Joan Mills. Playing time 60 minutes.

English Folk Guitar 2
Michael Raven
Price £7.50
This book is devoted to solo instrumental playing and in particular to styles developed from medieval lute and harp traditions. There are 37 tunes - the Cobbler, Cushion Dance, Adson's Sarabande, Drums of Johore, Maid of Provence, Glendower's Jig, Dove's Figary, Hills of Glenorchy, Road to Lisdoonvarna, etc. All the music is printed in tablature and staff notation. Most are not at all difficult and being such good and timeless tunes are rewarding to work on. 64 pages A4 size. **Companion Cassette:** has a playing time of 58 minutes.

English Folk Guitar 3
Michael Raven
Price £7.50
Like book 2 this is devoted entirely to solo instrumental pieces, 31 in all. Included are the concert solos: Black is the Colour and The Miller's Song by Michael Raven, The Little Heathy Hill by Nic Jones, The Siege of Delhi by Martin Carthy, and a good selection of jigs, reels, aires and morris dance tunes. All the music is in tablature and staff notation. 64 pages, A4 size. **Companion cassette:** all the music exactly as printed in the book except the Siege of Delhi and the Little Heathy Hill. Playing time 56 minutes.

English Folk Guitar 4
Michael Raven
Price £7.50
Transcriptions of all the guitar solos, songs and accompaniments on the CD *Recital*. Titles include: Lass from the Low Country, Ruth Ellis, Fortune My Foe, Dancing Delilah, Raglan Road, Bikers' Song, Welsh tunes and English traditional songs. 28 pieces in all. Most of the music is in both staff notation and tablature. 64 pages, 9 x 12 inches. **Companion CD:** 80 minutes duration.

Popular Music for Guitar
Michael Raven
Price £7.50
Contains a selection of 36 well known tunes in easy to moderately difficult arrangements - the Eton Boating Song, Schubert's Serenade, Cwm Rhondda, Fur Elise, Bluebell Polka, Crimond, Claire de Lune,
O Sole Mio, As I Went to Walsingham, Daisy Bell etc. The foreword suggests ways of using short tunes to make extended pieces. All the music is printed in both staff notation and tablature. 64 pages, A4 size.
Companion Cassette: contains performances of all the music in the book. Playing time 54 minutes.

Popular Classics for Guitar
Michael Raven
Price £7.50
Carefully selected to be within the range of the average player the contents are: 24 studies by
Carcassi; three gavottes by J.S. Bach, three renaissance lute pieces (all recorded by Julian Bream); Suite in D and Suite in E by Michael Raven; Maria Eleanor; English aires and dances and studies by Sor, Guilliani and Carulli. All the music is in staff notation and about half is also in tablature. 64 pages, A4 size.
Recording: there is not a companion cassette but some of the music has been recorded by Michael Raven on the LP (and cassette) A Miscellany of Guitar Music which is still available.

Easy Duets for Guitar
Joseph Kuffner
Price £4.50
In his day Joseph Kuffner (1776 1856) was the most celebrated composer in Europe, eclipsing even his illustrious friend Beethoven.
These easy duets are very easy indeed, yet musically most rewarding. What is more the top line stands complete as a solo composition. Printed here are Opus 80 and Opus 87 complete with a biography of Kuffner. These 37 duets are the best of their kind. There is no Companion cassette. 32 pages, A4

Recuerdos de la Alhambra
Francisco Tarrega
Price £3.00
Probably the most famous guitar solo ever written and not likely to be surpassed. The haunting melody is played using tremolo and the piece is technically difficult. Staff notation, tablature and chord diagrams There are photographs of the Alhambra, a Moorish palace in Granada, Spain, and a biography of the composer. Almost every leading guitarist has recorded this piece. 12 pages, A4.

Michael Raven:
Guitar Music 1 and 2
Michael Raven
Price £10.00
Books 1 and 2 in one volume. 76 pieces which include a grand concert solo arrangement of Bobby Shaftoe in gipsy style; arrangements of traditional tunes

such as Little Birds of the Mountain, Slaughter House and the English Echo; and new pieces such as Kellman's Harp, the Ratchup Pipes and Rag in G major. All in staff notation and tablature. 128 pages, 9 inches x 12 inches. **Companion Cassettes:** all the music note for note as written has been recorded on two 60 minute cassettes, one for each book, They can be ordered separately.

Michael Raven:
Guitar Music 3 and 4
Michael Raven
Price £10.00
Books 3 and 4 in one volume. 68 pieces which include Gipsy Part Two, a performance piece incorporating folk tunes and flamenco; English traditional dances, Irish polkas, new music and arrangements of popular songs such as Ain't She Sweet, Mendeissohn's Wedding March and a full notation of the Lichfield Bower Greenhill Processional, Mike Raven's best known concert solo. All in staff notation and tablature. 128 pages,
9 inches x 12 inches. **Companion Cassettes:** all the music note for note as written has been recorded on two 60 minute cassettes, one for each book. They can be ordered separately.

Music for Guitar
Michael Raven
Price £12.00
"A Magnum Opus." Charles Scott *Classical Guitar*. 155 easy to moderately difficult arrangements of a variety of music: lute pieces, popular songs, flamenco, folk tunes, country dances, original compositions etc. and some full concert solos. Titles include: Clun Castle Dirge, Carminda's Aire, Slain in Egypt, Colombiana, Pradoe Pavan, Black Queen, Jota, Tanguillio, Earl's Entry, Dead of Rajistan, Stockport Carnival Dance, etc. Note: this is not a compilation of previously published music. 256 pages, 9 x 12 inches, sewn in sections. **Companion Cassettes:** Five cassettes, £4.00 each. The recordings were made using my oid Ramirez flamenco guitar and a synthesised guitar.

An English Collection 1
Michael Raven
Price £2.50
11 pieces for solo guitar. Titles include: Off to California, Jigg Ashling, Beatrice Hill's Reel, Dowland's Alman etc. Easy to moderate; staff notation and tablature; 16 pages, A4.

Silent Field
Michael Raven
Price £7.50
36 pieces for solo guitar. Titles include: Mandrake, Mexican Serenade, Mills of Strata Marcella, Roaring Hornpipe, Jockey to the Fair, Mulberry Garden etc. and there are 14 Playford dances, 6 new pieces, 3 Scottish dances, 2 Flemish Maying songs and the famous Autumn Leaves. Easy to moderate; Staff notation and tablature, 64 pages; 9 x 12 inches.**Companion Cassette:** 63 minutes duration.

Star of Belle Isle
Michael Raven
Price £7.50
44 titles for solo guitar. Contents include: Four Short Pieces; Popular Songs (Don't Bring Lulu, Sicilian Waltz, etc.); Celtic Tunes: Flowers of the Forest, Wicklow Hornpipe, She Moves Through the Fair, etc; 17thC and 18thC Dances; and 16 English Country Dances (Abbot's Bromley Horn Dance etc.) Easy to moderate; staff notation and tablature; 64 pages, 9x12 inches. **Companion Cassette:** 69 minutes playing time.

Soulton Hall
Michael Raven
Price £7.50
36 aires, dances and cafe songs for solo guitar by Michael Raven from English country dances to Latin American pieces. Titles include: Cafe Song in E minor, Wolf's Head Polka, Christmas at Soulton Hall, Severn Boating Song, Watling Street Rag, Cajun Exile, Cadfael's Chant etc. Staff notation and tablature; 64 pages, 9x1 2 inches.
Companion Cassette: Duration 60 minutes.

Delbury Dervish
Michael Raven
Price £7.50
36 pieces for solo guitar comprising: 14 hymns (Richmond, Zachary, Eternal Father, Gonfalon Royal, etc.); 9 Thomas Hardy fiddle tunes arranged as The Dorchester Suite (Laura, Irish Devil, Speed the Plough, Volage Quadrille, etc.); and 13 Cafe Songs and Country Dances (Bringewood Waters, A49 Reel. Lazy Jane, etc.). Staff notation and tablature; 64 pages, 9x12 inches. **Companion Cassette:** 60 minutes duration.

Wizard Beguildy
Michael Raven
Price £7.50
35 English aires and country dances for solo guitar. Titles include: Argeers, Horsehay Two Stick Dance, Rosebud in June, Cat Tails Polka, Nutting Girl, Cherry Garden, Shirlett Forest Reels, Two French Brawls etc. and a curiosity, Freight Train as a flamenco waltz. Staff notation and tablature; 64 pages; 9x12 inches. **Companion Cassette:** 59 minutes.

Lucy's Frolic
Michael Raven
Price £7.50
35 aires and dances for solo guitar. Titles include: Badger Two Step, Clun Forest Dirge, Bathsheba's Hymn, Blackbird Fly No More, Lark in the Clear Air, Morrison's Jig, Confess, Lord Anson For Ever, Ode to Lydia etc. and a flamenco Garrotin (transcribed from the Guitar Magic LP). Staff notation and tablature; 64pages; 9x12 in. **Companion Cassette:** 55 minutes duration.

Songs and Solos
Michael Raven
Price £7.50
Transcriptions from the CD of all 24 guitar solos and 6 of the 13 songs (sung

by Joan Mills) and their accompaniments. Tunes include: Nottingham Swing, Mainstone Hornpipe, Newcastle (what a good tune that is), Lament for Peter Bellamy and Fred Jordan's Galliard. Amongst the songs are: Flowers in Her Hair, Octopus Dancing, Lament for Owain Glyndwr, Land of Lost Content, Mirror of My Mind and Midnight in the City etc. Staff notation and tablature; 64 pages,9 x 12 inches. **Companion CD:** 80 minutes duration. One guitar (steel strung Lowden) and one voice.

Welsh Guitar
Michael Raven
Price £7.50
Transcriptions from the CD of all 42 Welsh aires, dances and harp pieces arranged for solo guitar. Easy to moderate difficulty. Titles include: Grey Cuckoo, Sailor's Grave, Sweet Richard, Lady Treffael's Conceit, Spanish Minuet, Missing Boat, Watching the Wheat, John Francis, Lark's Elegy, etc. Michael Raven was born in Cardiff and went to school at Towyn. Staff notation and tablature; 64 pages, 9x12 inches. **Companion CD:** 70 minutes.

A Shropshire Lad
Michael Raven
Price £7.50
Transcriptions from the CD of all 20 Welsh aires and dances arranged for solo guitar and all 17 Housman poems set to traditional melodies (sung by Joan Mills). Some lovely and unusual music. Solos include: Megan's Daughter, Rhoslan Reel, White Rose of Summer, Clover, Farewell to Llangyfelach and Galaru etc. Most of Housman's best loved verses are here: Bredon Hill, On Wenlock Edge, Midnights of November, Is My Team Ploughing, Shrewsbury Jail etc. Solos and song accompaniments in staff notation and tablature; 64 pages; 9x12 inches. **Companion CD** 80 min. duration.

FOLK MUSIC

A Minstrel's Delight
Michael Raven
Price £10.00
An anthology of songs, country dances and concert guitar solos mostly transcribed from three CDs: The Reynardine Tapes, Taming the Dragon's Strings and Flowers of Picardy, performed by Michael Raven and Joan Mills. The songs include Old Dublin Fireman, Cypress Curtain of the Night, Erroll Flynn and Loveliest of Trees the Cherry Now, etc. Concert solos include Lovely on the Water and Spanish Morris, and there are traditional dance tunes such as Lady Coventry's Minuet and the Road to Lisdoonvarna, and some lovely Welsh 'listening music'. 96 pages, 9x12 inches, section sewn.

1,000 English Country Dance Tunes
Michael Raven
Price £20.00
The largest single collection of English country dance tunes ever published. Jigs, triple jigs, set dances, waltzes, reels, hornpipes, polkas, quicksteps, Schottisches etc., with special features on Morris. Sword and Ceremonial tunes, the Northumbrian pipes, and facsimile reproductions of the complete first editions of the Beggar's Opera (1729) and The English Dancing Master (1651). Widely acclaimed by professional folk and early music musicians. 224 pages, larger than A4 size.

Reynardine
Michael Raven
Price £7.50
This book contains a selection of music from the repertoire of a popular folk band. There are 72 pages of songs and dance tunes all of which are suitable for fiddle, flute, tin whistle, mandolin, bouzouki and guitar. The tunes are arranged in performance sets and many are printed complete with harmony lines and counter melodies. All have suggested harmonies indicated by chord symbols. The vocal music ranges from ancient ballads to industrial protest songs. The instrumental music includes jigs, reels, set dances, hornpipes, mazurkas, slides, polkas, aires and listening tunes, both traditional and newly composed. **Recordings:** some of the music has been recorded on The Reynardine Tapes CD.

Hynde Horn
Michael Raven
Price £7.50
A combined edition of two books: 'Ballads and Songs from Britain', and 'Aires and Dances of Wales'. Songs recorded by June Tabor, Steeleye Span and others, but also many little known traditional masterpieces and a handful of contemporary songs such as The Great Train Robbery, and Hyrmn to Che Guevara. 68 pages, A4 size.

A Shropshire Lad
A.E. Housman-Michael Raven
Price £3.00
A selection of 18 of Housman's poems set to some very fine traditional tunes by Michael Raven. Harmonies are suggested by chord symbols but most of these songs sound well unaccompanied. The First Edition is limited to 500 and the books (16 pages A4 size) are numbered and signed by Michael Raven.

Raven's Nest
Michael Raven
Price £4.50
Rural, industrial and contemporary folksongs, some with guitar accompaniment, all with chord symbols; 41 titles including a few poems and riddles: Bold Robin Hood, Stafford Pageant Song, Tim Evans' Dance, Darlaston Dogfight, My Last Farewell to Stirling, Wedgefield Wake, Queen of the Night, Midnight City,

Mirror of My Mind, Over the Wall, Brave Collier Lads. etc. 32 pages, A4 size. By using a condensed landscape format this book has almost twice the amount of material normally contained in a volume of this size and price. In short, it is a bargain! **Recordings:** There is not a Companion cassette but most of the songs have been recorded and details are given in the book.

Folksongs of the Low Countries
Michael Raven
Price £4.50
A collection of 20 songs and dance tunes from the Netherlands and Belgium with English translations. Each song tune has also been arranged as a guitar solo. There are some excellent tunes here - Leonore (recorded by Michael Raven on A Miscellany of Guitar Music, is especially attractive), Snow White Bird, Pierlala, and the Maying Song etc. The Belgian group, Rum, has also recorded some of these tunes. 32 pages, A4 size.

Kempion
Edited by David Oxley
and Michael Raven
Price £4.50
This book contains a collection of 30 mainly Irish and Scottish songs and dance tunes as played by a professional folk band. These are genuine off-the-record trans-criptions of actual performances, largely notated by members of the group themselves. All the music printed here has been tried and tested over many years of playing. The result is a first class collection of jigs, reels, hornpipes polkas and aires, arranged in performance sets and interspersed with songs and ballads. 32 pages, A4 size.

John O'Barbary
Michael Raven
Price £4.50
A collection of 32 traditional songs and dance tunes. Some are little known; some are from the repertoires of Silly Wizard, Nic Jones, June Tabor, The Bothy Band etc. Titles include, John O'Barbary, Tasman's Hunt, The Strayaway Child, Young Redin, The Wanton Seed, Jackie Tar, etc. The melody lines are in staff notation with chord symbols and there are some suggested harmonies and guitar accompaniments in tablature. 32 pages, A4 size.

The Jolly Machine
Michael Raven
Price £4.50
Sub-titled: 'Songs of Industrial Protest and Social Discontent from the West Midlands'. Contains some excellent but little known songs from the Potteries. Titles include: Waiting for Wages, The Tommy Note, Charlie's Song, The Nailmakers' Strike, The Dudley Boys etc. 32 pages, A4 size.
Companion CD: Many of the 23 songs have been recorded by Michael Raven and Joan Mills with Derby folk group Saga. See The Halliard : Jon Raven / Jolly Machine, CDMR77.

Victoria's Inferno
Jon Raven
Price £3.50
A unique collection of 72 songs of the old mines, mills, manufactories, canals and railways with comprehensive notes, full texts and melody lines with chord symbols. These 18th and 19th Century songs of colliers, cutlers, nailmakers, potters, shipwrights and railmen etc. were mostly written at times of strike, strife or disaster and are as much a social statement as a collection of songs. Jon Raven is a leading authority on industrial folksongs. He is the author of many books on the subject, and has been a consultant on numerous radio and television programmes. 192 pages, paperback size.

Urban and Industrial Songs of the Black Country and Birmingham
Jon Raven
Price £15.00
A beautifully produced hardback book finely printed on quality laid paper. This work, an outstanding study in industrial folksong, was supported by grants from the Leverhulme Trust and West Midlands Arts. 129 songs with text that describes their historical and social setting by Jon Raven, indisputably the leading authority in this field. 258 pages, A5 clothbound hardback.

Tarlton's Jests
Edited by Michael Raven
Price £3.00
Richard Tarlton (d. 1588) was a humble Shropshire farm labourer who became famous throughout England as Queen Elizabeth I's Court Jester. He was also an actor, a musician and one of the country's finest swordsmen, a Master of Fence. Tarlton's Jests were published shortly after he died and were an instant best-seller, a phenomenon of the age. The modern reader will find much of the humour slight. Nevertheless the Jests are important as an adjunct to social studies of the time, especially of Shakespeare, who knew Tarlton well. This edition is a facsimile of the book published by the Shakespeare Society in 1844. The original 39 pages have been reproduced on 16 landscape A4 pages.

Ross Workhouse Songbook
Michael Raven
Price £6.50
Transcriptions of all the songs, guitar accompaniments, guitar solos, poems and viola tunes on the *Songs and Dances of Herefordshire* CD which has contributions from Pat and Roy Palmer. Includes lovely versions of Lowlands of Holland, Dives and Lazarus, Milkmaid's Song and Sheffield Park and some fine dance tunes such as Jack of the Green and Mr. Baskerville's Volt. Music in staff notation only. 48 pages, 9 x 12 inches.

RECORDER, FLUTE, AND TIN WHISTLE MUSIC

Popular Songs for Recorder 1
Michael Raven
Price £2.00
These 32 tunes were carefully chosen to have lasting appeal - All around my Hat, Guantanamera, The Entertainer, Lord of the Dance, Wooden Heart, Green Leaves of Summer, Portsmouth, Return to Sorrento, Morning has Broken, Amazing Grace, In an English Country Garden etc. Breathing points are marked and chord symbols are given. This little book is attractive to young people and has been in print since 1977. It has 32 pages, A5 size.

Popular Songs for Recorder 2
Michael Raven
Price £4.00
The music is written a little larger than usual to help young people. Amongst the 46 tunes are:
A Policeman's Lot, Because You're Mine, El Condor Pasa, Malaguenia, Mexican Hat Dance, Sloop John B, Viva Espana, Whisky in the Jar Z Cars, Jamaica Farewell, A Bunch of Thyme, Onedin Line Theme etc. Chord symbols are printed above the melody lines and there is a descant recorder note chart. 32 pages, A4 size.

Popular Tunes for Recorder *Michael Raven*
Price £4.00
Also most suitable for the flute and the tin whistle. Indeed there is a full explanation of how the non-music reader can entabulate staff notation for the tin whistle. The contents include the Dark Island (Band of the Black Watch), March of Brian Boru, (James Galway), Morning Dew (Steeleye Span), Black Waterside (Led Zeppelin), Sonny Brogan's Mazurca (The Chieftains), Masters of War (Bob Dylan), Cuckoo's Nest (Albion Dance Band), My Kindly Sweetheart (Silly Wizard) etc. 35 tunes in all, 32 pages, A4 size.

The Tin Whistle Tutor
Michael Raven
Price £3.50
Since it was first published in 1977 this book has established itself as the most thorough tutor for the humble tin whistle ever printed. The player is taught how to read music as well as the tin whistle. There are clear diagrams, note charts, and also instruction on ornamentation and entabulation. Pieces to play include Sheebeg Sheemor, Give Me Your Hand and Aymara Indian Dance. 32 pages, A4 size.

RECORDINGS

A Shropshire Lad (CD)
Michael Raven (guitar)
Joan Mills (vocals)
Price £11.00
An 80 minute CD. 17 Housman poems, set to traditional melodies, alternate with 20 Welsh tunes arranged for solo guitar. Released 1994. A companion book is available.

Songs and Solos (CD)
Michael Raven (guitar)
Joan Mills (vocals)
Price £11.00
An 80 minute CD. 24 guitar solos and 13 songs. Released in 1994. Traditional and contemporary. "Quite exceptional", Nick Beale, *Folk Roots*. A companion book is available. See under Guitar Music.

The Dutch Connection
Michael Raven (guitar)
Joan Mills (vocals)
Price £6.50
Side One was recorded in Holland. Contents: Katie Cruel, Maid of Tottenham, Owain Glyndwr, Tenpenny Bit, Mad Tom of Bedlam, Constant Lovers, Clerk Colville, Young Jane, Lord McDonald, Burning of Auchindown, Brisk Young Widow, Miller's Song, Come Live with Me, Rogue's Wedding, Night Visiting Song, Improvisation, Ludlow Recruit, Rex Gloria, Robin Hood and the Tanner, Little Birds of the Mountain, Tarbolton Lodge,Longford Collector, Sailor's Bonnet, etc. (The last four titles with Reynardine.) 60 rninutes playing time. Available as cassette only.

The Folk Heritage Recordings
Michael Raven (guitar)
Joan Mills (vocals & guitar)
Price £6.50
Selected tracks from the LP Death and the Lady (1972): Jolly Highwayman, Lisa Lan, Ladies Don't Go a Thieving, Robin Hood's Dance, Sarabande, Captain's Apprentice, Can y Melinydd, Troseg y Gareg, Sarah Collins, White Gloves, La Russe Waltz, Paris Polka, Queen of the Night. Selected tracks from the LP Hymn to Che Guevara (1974): Belle Star and Jesse James, Twenty Years, Melancholy Pavan, Hymn to Che Guevara, Great Train Robbery Magpies in Picardy, Little White Donkey, Dancing Lady, Midnight City. 60 minutes playing time. Available as cassette only.

A Miscellany of Guitar Music
Michael Raven
Price £ 6.50
Recorded in 1977 on the Broadside Label. Contents: Suite in D: Prelude, Warrior's Welcome Home, Comical Fellow, Bushes and Briars, Two Butchers; Leonore, Aymara McKinnon's Lament and Jig, New Mown Hay, Bourree, Rough Music. Suite in E: Sarabande, Fanfare, Hymn Waltz; Lakes of Pontchartrain Jonathan Wild's Jig, Tarantos, Black Joke, To the Weavers. Available as either LP record or cassette.

Recital (CD)
Michael Raven and Joan Mills
Price £11
CDMR70. Duration 79 minutes. 14 traditional and contemporary songs and 12 guitar solos, which include Lass from the Low Country, Ruth Ellis, Raglan Road, Pavan for a Dead Princess, Black is the Colour and Illic Jacet All the music is in *English Folk*

Guitar 4. "Classic performances." Derek Gifford.

Songs and Dances of Herefordshire (CD)
Michael Raven (guitar) and Joan Mills (vocals) with guests Pat and Roy Palmer
Price £ 11.00
CDMR76. Duration 79 minutes. 16 songs, 10 guitar solos, 3 viola tunes and 4 poems. Some enchanting music, most of it previously unrecorded. Many of the songs were collected at the Ross Workhouse, demolished in 1995. All the music on the CD is printed in the *Ross Workhouse Songbook.*

Flowers of Picardy (CD)
Michael Raven (guitar mandolin, synthesizer, cittern, tambourine)
Joan Mills (vocals)
Price £ 11.00
CDMR73. Duration 77 minutes. 28 tracks. Titles include: Flowers of Picardy, Sicilian Waltz, Dancing Lady, Robin Hood's Dance, Trecynon Polka, Bentley Canal, Mallorca (by the Duke of Windsor), Oh Fair Enough and Epitaph on an Army of Mercenaries (Housman), Cypress Curtain of the Night (Campion) etc. Much of the music is in *A Minstrel's Delight,* due out in 1999.

Taming the Dragon's Strings (CD)
Michael Raven (guitar),
Joan Mills (guest vocal)
Price £11.00
CDMR71. Duration 71 minutes. 23 guitar solos, 2 Housman songs (The West, and Loveliest of Trees), and 21 original poems from *Song of the Fox* recited by Michael Raven. Guitar solos include the very popular Spanish Morris, Christmas at Soulton Hall, and Lovely on the Water. Amongst the poems are Foxy's Flying, Dark-haired Daughters and Pell Wall Hall.

|The Reynardine Tapes (CD)
Michael Raven (guitar, cittern, mandolin, bass, organ); Joan Mills (vocal, guitar, drum); John Rose (fiddle); Ado Morris (tin whistle, guitar)
Price £11.00
CDMR72. Duration 75 minutes. 22 tracks, 10 with Reynardine recorded In 1979. Songs and lively dance tunes. Titles include the band versions of Queen of the Night, Hungarian Hat, and Three Hearty Young Poachers, and the increasingly popular Old Dublin Fireman recorded by Mike and Joan in 1995. There are also two concert guitar solos - the Lichfield Bower Processional, and the epic Tarantos.

The Halliard : Jon Raven/ The Jolly Machine (CD)
Nic Jones, Dave Moran, Nigel Pattison, Mike Raven & Joan Mills with Saga (2 LP reissue)
Price £12.00
CDMR77. Duration 79 minutes. This CD is a slightly modified re-issue of two LP records. The Halliard : Jon Raven (Broadside BRO 106), first issued in 1968, was made for the

Halliard's farewell tour and contains some of their best known songs: Going for a Soldier Jenny, Lancashire Lads, Calico Printer's Clerk, and Ladies Don't Go a Thieving, etc. Two tracks from The Black Country Three (Transatlantic TRA 140) have been included. The Jolly Machine (Folk Heritage FHR 053) was recorded by Michael Raven and Joan Mills with Derby group Saga in 1974. All the songs are in the Jolly Machine book. The Black Country Three end the proceedings with the Dudley Canal Tunnel Song. 29 tracks in all.

Celtic Flamenco
Michael Raven (guitar)
Price £6.50
MR78 A cassette consisting of tracks taken from CD recordings of flamenco and flamenco inspired arrangements of British tunes. 38 minutes playing time.

The Irish In Me
Joan Mills (vocals)
with Michael Raven (guitar)
Price £6.50
MR79 Joan's mother, Margaret "Jeannie" Meehan, came from Ballindrait, Donegal. The contents are: Maid from the Northlands, Errol Flynn, Sally Gardens, The Backwoodsman, Old Dublin Fireman, Johnny Gallagher, Moorlough Shore. Widow Woman's Daughter, Brink of the White Rock, Star of Belle Isle, Irish Girl, Raglan Road. 46 minutes playing time. Cassette only.

My Old Friend
Michael Raven and Joan Mills with guest Johnny Collins
Price £12
CDMR80 Five guitar solos – Abbot's Bromley Horn Dance, Sheba's Daughter, Squire Mytton's Gallop, Grey Valley, and Spanish Morris – and 13 songs, almost all by Mike Raven: My Old Friend (for a much missed dog called Pirate), Errol Flynn, Song for Diana, Che Guevara (once released as a single), Is My Dear Lord Asleep? English Lanes, John Collins, Rebel Leader's Lament, Maid from the Northlands, My Bonny Lads Away, Loveliest of Trees. All the music and words of the songs and transcriptions of all the guitar solos are printed in a 36 page booklet which comes free with the CD. This highly acclaimed recording was released in 1998. Duration: 60 mins.

POETRY

Song of the Fox
Michael Raven
Price £2.50
A collection of 83 original songs, ballads and poems by Michael Raven. Titles include: Lines on Gatley Park, Sons of Glyndwr (from which was derived the name of a Welsh nationalist party), Song of the Fox, Why oh Wye? Dark-haired Daughters, Little Sparrow, Down in South Australia, Foxy's Flying, I am a Rabbit, etc. Second Edition with many new poems added. 64 pages, 4.5x7 inches paperback. LFQP